insight text guide

Grace Moore

Wuthering Heights

Emily Brontë

First published in 2011, reprinted 2012, 2013, 2014, 2015 (twice), 2016, 2020.

Insight Publications Pty Ltd
3/350 Charman Road
Cheltenham VIC 3192
Australia
Tel: +61 3 8571 4950
Fax: +61 3 8571 0257
Email: books@insightpublications.com.au

www.insightpublications.com.au

National Library of Australia Cataloguing-in-Publication entry:
Moore, Grace, 1974-
Emily Bronte's Wuthering Heights / Grace Moore.
9781921411861 (pbk.)
For secondary school age.
Bronte, Emily, 1818-1848 Wuthering Heights
Bronte, Emily, 1818-1848—Criticism and interpretation.
823.8

Other ISBNs:
9781925175806 (digital)
9781925175813 (bundle: print + digital)

Cover design: The Modern Art Production Group

Printed in Australia by Ligare

contents

CHARACTER MAP

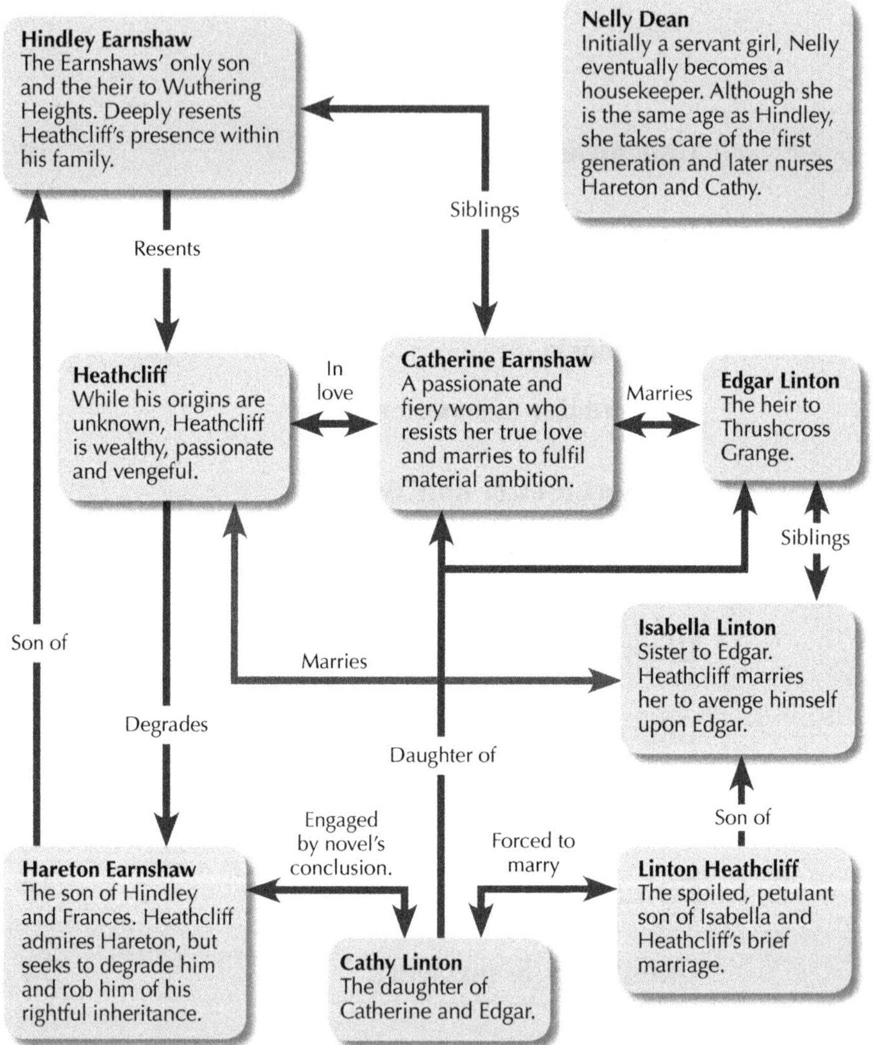

OVERVIEW

About the author

Emily Brontë was born in Thornton, Yorkshire in 1818. In 1820 her father, the Reverend Patrick Brontë, became the curate of Haworth, also in Yorkshire. Emily spent much of her life in the area, which provides the setting for *Wuthering Heights*. The sister of novelists Anne and Charlotte Brontë, Emily was painfully shy and, while a great deal is known of Charlotte's life, Emily poses much more of a challenge to biographers. She does not seem to have made friends beyond her family, nor has she left behind many documents offering clues to her life. Lucasta Miller comments that the 'absences surrounding her have made her all the more magnetic', noting that a large number of myths have circulated around her life (Miller 2001, p.171).

Emily Brontë's upbringing was, like that of her sisters, somewhat haphazard. Her mother died when she was three years old and her aunt, Elizabeth Branwell, moved into the parsonage to help raise the Brontë children. In November 1824, at the age of six, Emily was sent to join her sisters, Charlotte, Maria and Elizabeth, at Cowan Bridge, a boarding school for daughters of the clergy. It is believed that the harsh regime at Lowood School in Charlotte Brontë's *Jane Eyre* (1847) was modelled on this school. A poor diet allowed illness to flourish and, as Juliet Barker notes, out of the fifty-three pupils who attended the school at the same time as the Brontës, one died at the school and six of the eleven others sent home because of illness died shortly thereafter (Barker 2010, p.147). Emily's sisters Maria and Elizabeth became ill while attending the school, with Maria dying of consumption in May 1825 and Elizabeth succumbing to the same disease in June of that year. Emily and Charlotte were removed from the school on 1 June 1825, and Emily did not attend school again until 1835, when she accompanied Charlotte (who was to work there as a teacher) to Roe Head School, 18 miles from Haworth.

During the years she spent at home, Emily had joined her surviving sisters and their brother, Branwell, in creating imaginary worlds and writing stories about these worlds and their inhabitants. While Charlotte and Branwell worked together on adventures in 'Angria', Emily and Anne created the world of 'Gondal' together. Away from Anne, Emily seems to have missed the stimulation of the Gondal saga and, finding it difficult to submit to the structured routine of school life, she returned to the parsonage after just three months at Roe Head (Barker 2010, pp.274–75). Emily continued to produce stories of Gondal into her twenties and they formed an important part of her apprenticeship as a writer.

At the age of twenty, she took a position as a teacher at Law Hill School in Halifax, but ill health and her ongoing difficulty with the routine and discipline of school life caused her to relinquish the post within seven months. Emily wrote a number of poems during this time, as well as pieces associated with Gondal. Juliet Barker notes that the poems Emily produced during this period were among her best (Barker 2010, p.346).

Emily left home again in 1842, this time travelling with Charlotte to Brussels, where they planned to improve their French and German. Their intention was to open a school together on their return to Haworth. Supported by a loan from their aunt, they attended the Pensionnat Heger, spending six months there as pupils. They were invited to remain for an additional six months, with Charlotte offering English classes and Emily teaching music, in exchange for board and language lessons. According to Charlotte, Emily found this period difficult, but she worked hard to overcome her customary homesickness and remained in Brussels until November, when they learned of their aunt's death. While Charlotte eagerly returned to Belgium the following year, Emily remained at home.

Emily's literary success might not have occurred at all if Charlotte had not discovered a notebook containing her poems in the autumn of 1845. Emily was furious at the violation of her privacy and initially resisted Charlotte's urge to publish them. The poems eventually appeared alongside verses by Anne and Charlotte, published under a pseudonym in 1846 as *Poems by Currer, Ellis, and Acton Bell*. The sisters chose masculine names in the hope that their works would be taken more seriously. From this point onwards, scholars believe that Emily was working on *Wuthering Heights*, but there is little she has left behind to tell us of the creative process. The novel was published in 1847, with Emily once again using her 'Ellis Bell' *nom de plume*. The work appeared with Anne's novel, *Agnes Grey*, but it was Emily's book that attracted a significant degree of controversy and criticism. The original and intense *Wuthering Heights* was to be Emily's only novel. Having suffered from consumption for some time, Emily Brontë died at the age of thirty on 19 December 1848.

Synopsis

Regarded by many readers as one of the greatest love stories, *Wuthering Heights* is also a tale of revenge and deception. The story begins with Lockwood's visit to Wuthering Heights, a house owned by his landlord, Heathcliff. Forced by bad weather to spend the night at the Heights, Lockwood is either haunted by or dreams of the ghost of Catherine Earnshaw. Returning to Thrushcross Grange, the house he is renting, Lockwood quizzes the housekeeper, Nelly Dean, who agrees to tell him Heathcliff's story.

When old Mr Earnshaw brings a dark-skinned orphan, Heathcliff, home, his son Hindley is jealous and takes a dislike to the boy. Heathcliff becomes a favourite not only with Mr Earnshaw, but also with Hindley's sister, Catherine. Upon Mr Earnshaw's death, Hindley takes revenge on Heathcliff by reducing him to the position of a servant. Catherine and Heathcliff remain close, but one Sunday, while they are watching an argument between Edgar Linton and his sister, Isabella, at nearby Thrushcross Grange, Catherine is seriously injured. Remaining at the Grange for several weeks, Catherine grows accustomed to its comforts and returns home with an air of refinement. In the meantime, Heathcliff has been forbidden to consort with her, although the pair still spend time together in secret.

Tempted by a life of wealth and leisure at the Grange, Catherine accepts a marriage proposal from Edgar Linton, despite her love for Heathcliff. She attempts to explain her decision to Nelly Dean, a servant at the time. Overhearing part of the discussion, Heathcliff learns that Catherine believes it would degrade her to marry him. He disappears and Catherine, frantic at his loss, falls ill. Three years later, when Catherine is married to Edgar Linton, Heathcliff returns, wealthy and refined. Much to Edgar's annoyance, Catherine is overjoyed to see him. Catherine falls ill once again, refusing to eat and seeking to punish her husband by making herself sick. Heathcliff elopes with Isabella Linton in order to anger her brother, Edgar. He does not love her and is so brutal that Isabella later escapes from him and moves to the south of England, where she raises their son, Linton. Heathcliff later returns to the Grange to see Catherine, and the shock to her nervous system kills her, just two hours after she has given birth to her daughter, Cathy.

The second half of the novel is largely concerned with the next generation and Heathcliff's efforts to enact his vengeance upon the descendants of both the Lintons and Hindley Earnshaw. Heathcliff gains possession of Wuthering Heights by taking advantage of Hindley's drinking and gambling. When Hindley dies, Heathcliff attempts to degrade his son, Hareton, in revenge for the treatment he received as a youth.

Cathy Linton grows up in ignorance of the drama involving her parents and Heathcliff. It is not until her aunt Isabella dies and Edgar brings her cousin, Linton, to the Grange that she gradually becomes aware of Heathcliff and his desire to cause pain to Edgar and his family. Heathcliff demands that Linton be handed over to him and Edgar complies. Cathy later escapes from the confines of the Grange and learns that Linton is living a matter of miles away. She begins a sequence of secret visits to him and, eventually, when her father is on his deathbed, Heathcliff forces her to marry his son, Linton, who is also on the brink of death, so that he may claim her property.

Cathy is left penniless and is compelled to live at Wuthering Heights, where Lockwood, Heathcliff's tenant and one of the story's narrators, meets her. A year later, Lockwood returns to hear the end of the story and to find Heathcliff dead – having lost his impetus for revenge – and Cathy and Hareton engaged to be married.

Character summaries

Catherine Earnshaw (Linton): a headstrong, passionate young woman who refutes her love for her foster brother, Heathcliff, to satisfy her social ambition by marrying Edgar Linton.

Catherine (Cathy) Linton (Heathcliff): Catherine and Edgar's daughter, Cathy leads a secluded life at Thrushcross Grange until she ventures forth to Wuthering Heights and becomes embroiled in Heathcliff's revenge plot.

Ellen Dean (Nelly): the housekeeper at Wuthering Heights and Thrushcross Grange, as well as the narrator of much of the story. Nelly has grown up with the Earnshaws and is unsympathetic towards the first Catherine, often making judgemental comments about her and bemoaning her fiery temper. Nelly also withholds information about Catherine's health from her husband, Edgar.

Frances Earnshaw: Hindley's young, delicate wife, who dies of consumption shortly after giving birth to their son, Hareton.
Hareton Earnshaw: the son of Hindley and Frances Earnshaw, Hareton is degraded by Heathcliff and robbed of his rightful inheritance.
Mr Earnshaw: the father of Catherine and Hindley, he brings Heathcliff home with him following a trip to Liverpool and makes the boy a favourite.
Mrs Earnshaw: Catherine and Hindley's mother.
Heathcliff: brought home from Liverpool by old Mr Earnshaw, Heathcliff's true origins are never known. Resented by Hindley, Heathcliff is forced to undertake the work of a servant when Hindley becomes the head of the household. Passionately devoted to Catherine Earnshaw, Heathcliff devotes his life to vengeance on the houses of Earnshaw and Linton after her death.
Linton Heathcliff: Heathcliff and Isabella Linton's son. A weak, spoiled and petulant boy he, on his father's insistence, marries Cathy Linton.
Hindley Earnshaw: Catherine's brother, Hindley is jealous of Heathcliff from the outset and, when Mr Earnshaw dies, he takes revenge by forcing Heathcliff to do the work of a menial labourer.
Joseph: deeply religious and highly judgemental, Joseph is a servant at the Heights, notable for his unforgiving nature and his broad Yorkshire accent.
Edgar Linton: a spoiled boy, Edgar grows to love Catherine Earnshaw. Although he is cowardly in his interactions with Heathcliff, he grows into a responsible, likeable character who, while mourning Catherine's death, loves and cares for their daughter, Cathy.
Isabella Linton: Edgar's younger sister, an indulged young woman who elopes with Heathcliff in spite of warnings from both Heathcliff and Catherine.
Mr and Mrs Linton: Edgar and Isabella's parents. A generous couple, they both fall ill and die from an illness that Catherine Earnshaw brings into the household.
Lockwood: the story's narrator. Seeking to retreat from society, Lockwood rents Thrushcross Grange from Heathcliff and falls ill soon after his arrival. Seeking a diversion during his convalescence, he asks Nelly Dean to tell him the history of the people he meets at Wuthering Heights.
Zillah: a housekeeper at Wuthering Heights.

BACKGROUND AND CONTEXT

In her introduction to the Penguin edition of *Wuthering Heights*, Lucasta Miller suggests that the world of the novel was, like Emily Brontë's own world, 'hermetically sealed' (p.xvi). It is striking that, at a time when the novel was increasingly engaged with issues of social reform, Brontë's characters and the drama unfolding around them seem to be isolated from the wider world. Part of the novel's remarkable intensity stems from its focus on the worlds of Wuthering Heights and Thrushcross Grange, generating what is at times almost a state of claustrophobia in its exclusion of everything except the stormy emotions of the central protagonists.

Brontë's context is, however, more important to our understanding of the novel than might at first appear. The most influential account of the Brontës' lives to appear in the nineteenth century was Elizabeth Gaskell's *The Life of Charlotte Brontë* (first published 1857). Gaskell was a friend of Charlotte's in her later life and attempted, through her biography, to offset charges of coarseness made against the sisters by depicting them as the unworldly inhabitants of a remote backwater with 'peculiar forms of population and society' (Gaskell 1997, p.8) and where drunkenness was rife. However, Haworth, where the sisters grew up, was a thriving industrial area, close to the large manufacturing cities of Bradford and Halifax, and containing a number of small woollen textile mills (Barker 2010, p.106). Terry Eagleton's comments that the Brontës 'happened to live in a region which revealed the friction between land and industry in a peculiarly stark form' (Eagleton, 2005a, p.8), and where Chartism and other forms of political activism were widespread further contradict Gaskell's representation.

While it is certainly not a politically engaged novel, *Wuthering Heights* reflects some of the social and economic changes of the 1840s and the class tensions that accompanied them. The decline of the Earnshaw family, the assimilation of Hareton into the world of Thrushcross Grange and the abandonment of Wuthering Heights to 'such ghosts as may choose to inhabit it' (p.337) signal, according to critics including Arnold Kettle and Terry Eagleton, the demise of the yeoman farmer in the face of the social change sweeping across nineteenth-century Britain. While Wuthering Heights is a working farm, Thrushcross Grange represents the leisured environment enjoyed by the emerging middle classes. For Kettle, it is notable that just as Catherine Earnshaw was seduced by the comfort of an idle lifestyle at the Grange, by the end of the novel, Hareton Earnshaw is preparing to move there. The farm is left to waste, just as across the country people who had traditionally worked on the land were migrating to the cities in droves.

The novel certainly reflects Victorian concerns about the mysterious origin of fortunes that were, in an age of industrialism and financial speculation, often made and lost overnight. The source of the fortune that Heathcliff accumulates during his three-year absence remains unknown; the Heathcliff who returns from exile is so thoroughly wicked that almost any explanation is possible. However, the fact that he spends a great deal of time gambling with Hindley once he is ensconced at the Heights suggests that it may have been acquired through unscrupulous dealings in stocks and shares. As the cultural critic Franco Moretti has noted, representations of gambling in nineteenth-century novels are often evocative of a broader climate of risk and speculation (Moretti 1993, pp.130–56). The fact that Heathcliff seeks to win property, and not necessarily by fair means, would, for a Victorian reader, call to mind the tainted wealth and rapid accumulation of fortunes through currency trading and other risky ventures. That the origins of Heathcliff's money remain unknown makes his dealings all the more suspicious and, as readers, we are offered the opportunity to speculate on what Heathcliff may or may not have done during his three-year absence.

Heathcliff's early years are just as much a source of mystery as his absence as an adult, and recently his origins have been the subject of scrutiny by critics considering the novel in its colonial context. While Nelly Dean remarks that Heathcliff may be a 'prince in disguise' (p. 58) with origins in China or India, his birthplace may well have been somewhat closer to home. Although Emily Brontë's father, the Reverend Patrick Brontë, was educated at Cambridge, he was born into a poor family in Emdale, County Down, in Ireland. Patrick Brontë does not seem to have maintained contact with his Irish family after his move to mainland Britain and there is no evidence to suggest that Emily ever visited her father's homeland. However, Emily's Irish heritage offers one possible explanation for Heathcliff's origins and critics, including Mary Jean Corbett (2000) and Terry Eagleton (2005b), have argued that the orphaned Heathcliff, found wandering the streets of Liverpool, may in fact have been an Irish migrant.

The 1840s were known as the 'hungry forties' both in mainland Britain and in Ireland. It was a period of widespread starvation, partly because of tariffs on the price of corn, but largely because of the failure of potato crops across Europe. Ireland, where potatoes were a staple food, was particularly badly affected by the potato blight and the death toll from the resulting famine is believed to have been more than a million. Many people sought to escape hunger through migration, with Irish families settling in the US, Canada and Australia. A large number of migrants passed through the port of Liverpool, either as part of their longer journey across the globe or because they had chosen to settle in England to seek work in the large northern manufacturing towns.

While the plot of *Wuthering Heights* does not take place in the Britain of the 1840s, Brontë would have been conscious of an influx of Irish migrants, if not through first-hand experience, then certainly through the newspapers. Pointing to Catherine and Heathcliff's fascination with hunger and starvation, Terry Eagleton interprets the characters as representatives of the starving Irish. He argues that Heathcliff's incoherent chatter when he is rescued by old Mr Earnshaw is actually Gaelic and that he is a 'famished Irish immigrant (who) becomes a landless labourer set to work in the Heights' (Eagleton 1995, p.19). For Eagleton, Heathcliff's class ascent and his transformation into a brutal landlord mirrors the ways in which Irish farmers mimicked the behaviour of their English oppressors and eventually went on to dispossess them. Heathcliff thus abandons his childish idealism – losing sight of his love for Catherine – and becomes obsessed with revenge, turning himself into a 'predatory English landlord' (Eagleton 1995, p.20).

One of the most fascinating elements of *Wuthering Heights* is that just as it offers up a number of tantalising contextual readings, it also resists them through omissions and ambiguities. Emily Brontë's context, therefore, offers potential insights into the novel, but the work's richness comes from the many meanings and interpretations it has evoked.

GENRE, STRUCTURE & LANGUAGE

Genre

Wuthering Heights is one of the most original and innovative novels of the nineteenth century because of the way it brings together a variety of genres. In many ways utterly distinct from its literary predecessors, the work nevertheless incorporates aspects of realist writing, which would increasingly become the dominant mode for Victorian novelists seeking to make sense of the world around them by exploring it in fiction.

Realist writers attempt to create a world that *seems* real to readers even though the fictional world at times draws attention to its own artifice. In her guide to realist fiction, Pam Morris has identified *Wuthering Heights* as 'the novel that most radically draws upon romanticism, popular culture and multiple perspectives to undercut any epistemological certainty' (Morris 2003, p.81). Complicated though this analysis may sound, Morris is suggesting that Brontë has created a world that seems simultaneously real, yet not real. The shifting nature of the narrative enhances the reader's sense of suspense and prepares us to embrace the unexpected.

The novel's fusion of genres brings Gothic writing (an eighteenth-century mode famous for its melodrama and supernatural elements) together with a romance-based plot. The character of Heathcliff embodies these two extremes: on one level he is a realistic character, a landlord performing his daily work; yet, as we learn from Nelly, he can also be superhumanly evil and a devoted, but destructively passionate lover. These different perceptions of Heathcliff point us to the ambiguity at the centre of the novel and the dangers of attempting to place it in a single category.

A significant number of readers regard *Wuthering Heights* as primarily a love story. Indeed, in a recent survey by the UKTV drama channel, the novel was voted the greatest love story ever written, ahead of William Shakespeare's *Romeo and Juliet* and Jane Austen's *Pride and Prejudice*. However, the novel's emphasis on pain, suffering and vengeance means that it sits uncomfortably in the 'romantic fiction' category. While for some, Heathcliff may epitomise the dominant masculinity of a rebellious Byronic hero, other readers regard him as brutal and insensitive, the 'wolfish man' (p.103) of Catherine Earnshaw's description. This fascinating tension is another consequence of Brontë's mixing of genres, creating a multiplicity of responses from readers with different perspectives and backgrounds.

Its strong focus on nature means that *Wuthering Heights* is frequently identified as a novel reflecting the influence of the Romantic poets, including William Wordsworth and Samuel Taylor Coleridge. Emily Brontë's depiction of the natural world in her descriptions combines intense feelings with elaborate imagery, often using the weather or the landscape to reflect a character's feelings or to tell us something about their characteristics, such as when Catherine compares her love for Heathcliff to 'the eternal rocks beneath' (p.82).

Structure

An early anonymous review of *Wuthering Heights* that appeared in *The Examiner* on 8 January 1848 described the novel as 'wild, confused, disjointed, and improbable ... the worst-constructed tale that was ever written' (in Allott 1974, p.220). While this comment encapsulates some of the confusion experienced by the novel's first readers, it significantly downplays the complexities of Emily Brontë's elaborate plot and the demands it makes on the reader.

According to Peter Garrett, *Wuthering Heights* should be regarded as a 'multi-plot' novel because of the ways in which 'it plays double- against single-focus narrative' (Garrett 1980, p.221). Brontë presents her readers with a carefully structured narrative-within-a-narrative, which adds plausibility to some of the more supernatural elements of the plot by channelling them firstly through Nelly Dean and then through Lockwood, who recounts them to us without casting doubt on their veracity.

The narrative is arranged in two parts, with the first volume focusing on Catherine Earnshaw and Heathcliff's desperate love, and the second volume mostly focusing on the next generation and their struggles in the wake of Catherine's decision to marry Edgar. In chronological terms, the story does not always follow a strict linear pattern. In the opening chapters, it is interrupted several times by Lockwood's interjections about his health and his life as the tenant of Thrushcross Grange, but it is not so fractured that it is difficult to follow. The story is, however, slightly unsettling in that we have already met Hareton and Cathy as adults when Lockwood makes his first two visits to Wuthering Heights, which, while stimulating Lockwood's interest, also gives the reader the illusion of believing that he or she knows how the story will end. As it is, Brontë manages to subvert our expectations by removing Lockwood from the scene for a year, before allowing him to return to see Cathy and Hareton unexpectedly engaged to be married. Garrett argues that the novel 'traces a cycle of disruption and renewal' (Garrett 1980, p.223), interpreting the repetition of names in the novel's second half as an attempt to impose order upon a world that has been catastrophically disrupted. Terry Eagleton goes further and characterises the narrative style as akin to a set of Chinese boxes, 'in which one potentially unreliable narrative is embedded in another not entirely trustworthy one, and that perhaps within another' (Eagleton 2005b, p.136), arguing that any sense of stability we may gain is illusory.

The structure of *Wuthering Heights* is, like the novel itself, complex, unsettling and constantly shifting. Brontë's departure from the linear development that characterised more mainstream fiction demonstrates an original approach that defies the conventions of storytelling and aptly represents her subversive characters.

Language

By the 1840s, the English realist novel had become increasingly engaged with character and psychology, but the narrative mode of *Wuthering Heights* restricts our understanding of the central protagonists' motives and desires. Everything we know about the characters we meet is influenced by the biases and preconceptions of Nelly Dean and, to a lesser degree, Lockwood. This places us in a world where language is neither reliable nor authoritative and where we must constantly question the judgements offered to us, particularly by the confident, yet unreliable Nelly.

Nelly only once casts doubt upon herself, when she and Cathy are taken prisoner at the Heights. She tells us that she spent time, 'passing harsh judgment on my many derelictions of duty; from which, it struck me then, all the misfortunes of all my employers sprang' (p.276). While as readers we may agree with her assessment, Nelly is quick to dismiss it by continuing, 'It was not the case, in reality' (p.276). Having signalled her biases and petty jealousies throughout the story, particularly in relation to first-generation characters, such as Catherine and Heathcliff, this moment of uncertainty on Nelly's part is clearly designed to make us reconsider her role in events and to cast doubt on the truth of her words.

The narrative mode means that voice is extremely important in *Wuthering Heights*, even though all characters are mediated through Nelly and Lockwood. Brontë's use of language can be described as polyphonic. Literally meaning 'many sounds', the idea of polyphony in the novel refers to the way in which different voices vie with one another and jostle for our attention. Since characters change and some share names, their expressions and the cadences of their speech are important ways of distinguishing between people. Catherine and Heathcliff, for example, express themselves in dramatic (some would say melodramatic) and passionate forms, while Cathy and Linton are much more muted, as is exemplified by Cathy's 'very pretty and very silly' letters to Linton and the 'worthless trash' of his responses (p.225). Later on, of course, Heathcliff recognises that his son's notes are inadequate and interferes with his letter-writing (p.259), knowing that Linton's self-absorbed, complaining voice will neither satisfy Edgar's concerns nor attract Cathy. Joseph, on the other hand, makes himself memorable through his strong (and for some readers, impenetrable) Yorkshire dialect, which reminds us of the different life on the moors, his class difference and the radically different voices of the moor-dwellers.

By spurning an omniscient (all-knowing) narrator, Brontë denies herself the opportunity to voice her own moral judgements on her characters' behaviour and denies us deep insights into their thoughts and feelings. As a consequence, everything we hear is subjective and we are able to infer a character's state of mind only through the words they choose to utter. This technique creates a strange distance between us and the characters, whose voices and opinions are always at least two stages removed from us. In spite of this distancing effect, Brontë sought to convey the force of her characters' feelings through a more authentic language, as is demonstrated by her decision to depart from the practice of representing profanities with a dash, choosing instead to write the word in full. While this usage was shocking to a number of the novel's first readers, it represents a commitment to the realistic portrayal of characters' accents and emotional states.

CHAPTER-BY-CHAPTER ANALYSIS

Volume I, Chapter I (pp.3–8)

Summary: *Lockwood visits Wuthering Heights for the first time.*

We are introduced to Lockwood, the tenant of Thrushcross Grange, who has returned from a visit to Wuthering Heights. He recounts the curious household and offers his impressions of its occupants. Lockwood points to the house's exposure to the elements, noting that the surrounding stunted trees grow at a slant because the north wind (p.4). As we learn more about the Heights' occupants, the author invites us to draw a parallel between them, the turbulent weather and the misshapen trees.

Q Why does Lockwood draw parallels between himself and Heathcliff?

Volume I, Chapter II (pp.9–18)

Summary: *Lockwood returns to the Heights, although he has been told that he will be unwelcome.*

Despite Heathcliff's warning that he is not welcome at Wuthering Heights, Lockwood returns and, in doing so, demonstrates his fallibility as a judge of character, mood and northern weather. He is received inhospitably by Cathy, whom he erroneously believes to be Heathcliff's wife and, although warned against braving the weather to travel home, he attempts to leave. He is prevented from doing so by two ferocious dogs.

Q How does Emily Brontë make use of dogs to indicate character in the opening chapters?

Volume I, Chapter III (pp.19–32)

Summary: *Lockwood dreams of, or is haunted by, Catherine Earnshaw's ghost.*

Zillah, the housekeeper, leads Lockwood upstairs to a room, and asks him to conceal the fact that he is sleeping there from Heathcliff. Lockwood begins to read Catherine Earnshaw's diary, but falls asleep and dreams of her. It is never entirely clear, however, whether the experience is a dream or an encounter with a ghost. Lockwood's fearful cries attract Heathcliff's attention and he sends Lockwood away from the room. Lockwood then overhears Heathcliff sobbing to Catherine and begging her to come in.

Key point

Heathcliff throws open the window and, with unexpected passion, calls on Catherine to come in (p.28).

Q Do you think Lockwood's encounter with Catherine was a dream or a supernatural experience? Draw on the text to explain your response.

Volume I, Chapter IV (pp.33–40)

Summary: *Nelly begins to tell Heathcliff's story.*

Lockwood returns home and asks Nelly Dean to tell him more about Heathcliff. She recounts Heathcliff's past, from the moment of his arrival in the Earnshaw family, and emphasises the mystery surrounding his origins and the aversion Hindley feels towards him. Nelly also begins to reveal her partisanship as a narrator, making it clear that she held little affection for Catherine Earnshaw.

Key point

Mr Earnshaw brings the starving, homeless Heathcliff back to Wuthering Heights following his trip to Liverpool (p.37).

Q Consider how the layers of the narrative become more complicated with Lockwood recounting Nelly's version of events.

Volume I, Chapter V (pp.41–44)

Summary: *Mr Earnshaw dies.*

While Heathcliff and Catherine have become inseparable, Hindley resents the foundling, whom he sees as a rival, and is sent away to college. Catherine vexes her father with her mischievous behaviour and her obvious influence over Heathcliff. Mr Earnshaw dies, having made Heathcliff a favourite.

Q Do you think that Nelly's representation of Catherine is unbiased? Analyse Nelly's descriptions to support your response.

Volume I, Chapter VI (pp.45–52)

Summary: *Hindley returns with a wife. Catherine is wounded at Thrushcross Grange.*

Hindley returns home from college for his father's funeral and brings a wife, Frances, with him. Frances takes a dislike to Heathcliff and Hindley compels his rival to become an outdoor labourer. One Sunday evening, Heathcliff returns home without Catherine and reports that she has been attacked by a bulldog at Thrushcross Grange while watching Edgar and Isabella Linton squabble over a spoiled lapdog (note the contrast between the dog at the Grange and those at the Heights). Hindley is furious and forbids Heathcliff from speaking to Catherine when she returns from the Grange, where she spends five weeks recovering from her injuries.

Q How does life at Thrushcross Grange appear to differ from the world of Wuthering Heights?

Volume I, Chapter VII (pp.53–63)

Summary: *The Lintons are invited over for Christmas, causing tension at the Heights, particularly between Heathcliff and Edgar.*

Catherine returns to Wuthering Heights for Christmas. Hindley and Frances admire the refined behaviour Catherine has learned at the Grange, although her changes are only superficial and she retains her strong bond with Heathcliff. After Catherine thoughtlessly comments on her friend's dirtiness, Heathcliff asks Nelly to help him smarten up his appearance. The Lintons visit on Christmas Day and Heathcliff speaks to Nelly of his despair when he compares himself to Edgar. A skirmish breaks out between Heathcliff and Edgar, who are already becoming rivals, and Hindley removes Heathcliff from the festivities. Heathcliff confides to Nelly that he wishes to pay Hindley back for relegating him to the position of a servant.

Q How does Emily Brontë establish a contrast between Heathcliff and Edgar's characters in this chapter? Pay particular attention to the representation of masculinity.

Volume I, Chapter VIII (pp.64–73)

Summary: *Hareton Earnshaw is born and Frances dies. Catherine shocks Edgar with a characteristic display of violent temper.*

Hareton Earnshaw is born and Mr Kenneth informs Hindley that Frances will die. Hindley refuses to accept the diagnosis and, until the moment of her death, asserts that his wife will recover. Nelly is charged with raising Hareton and Hindley's behaviour spirals out of control. Edgar Linton visits and Catherine refuses to turn him away to spend time with the jealous Heathcliff. Catherine behaves violently towards Nelly and Hareton in front of Edgar, who is shocked. When he attempts to leave, Catherine strikes him. Nelly warns Edgar of Catherine's temper, but the quarrel brings the pair closer together.

Key point

Heathcliff shows Catherine the almanac on which he has marked the time Catherine spends with Edgar, compared to the time she spends with him (p.70).

Q Why does Catherine behave with such violence in this chapter? Think beyond her annoyance with Nelly.

Volume I, Chapter IX (pp.74–90)

Summary: *Heathcliff overhears Catherine comparing him to Edgar and disappears.*

Hindley drops Hareton over a banister and Heathcliff catches him. Catherine seeks out Nelly to discuss whether or not she should marry Edgar Linton. Nelly, who is emerging as a manipulative and meddlesome character, conceals Heathcliff's presence from Catherine, who is candid about her material ambitions. Heathcliff stays long enough to hear Catherine say that to marry him would degrade her; he then disappears. While looking for Heathcliff, Catherine is soaked in a storm that symbolises her emotional state. She falls ill of a fever that she passes on to Edgar's parents, who die from it. Three years later, Edgar and Catherine are married and Nelly is forced to leave Hareton behind and move to Thrushcross Grange.

Key point

Catherine compares her love for Heathcliff to her feelings for Edgar (pp.82–83). This is an important scene because it outlines the depth of the love she shares with Heathcliff as well as her social and material ambitions. It is also the catalyst for Heathcliff's departure and the tragedy that ensues.

Q Consider the role of dreams in the novel so far, paying particular attention to Catherine's dream of heaven (p.80).

Volume I, Chapter X (pp.91–107)

Summary: *Heathcliff returns unexpectedly.*

Lockwood is ill for a month and asks Nelly to distract him with more of the story. Nelly outlines the mystery of Heathcliff's newfound wealth and refinement, and explains Catherine's changed character after her illness, noting that she is always allowed to have her own way. Heathcliff returns unexpectedly and Catherine is ecstatic. Heathcliff explains that he had not planned to stay, but to see Catherine's face once, settle his score with Hindley and then leave. Edgar is unsettled by his rival's return and his changed bearing, while Nelly voices her concern that Heathcliff will be staying at the Heights with Hindley. Isabella begins to fall in love with Heathcliff and regards Catherine as a competitor for his affection.

Q Why is Isabella drawn to Heathcliff in spite of his gruff treatment of her?

Volume I, Chapter XI (pp.108–119)

Summary: *Catherine locks Heathcliff and Edgar in a room together.*

Nelly meets Hareton on her way to the Heights and is shocked when she learns that Heathcliff has taught the boy to curse. Hoping to meet Hindley, Nelly runs into Heathcliff instead and flees in terror. Heathcliff continues his flirtation with Isabella and, when Edgar hears of it, he decides to eject Heathcliff from the Grange. Edgar and Catherine argue, and Edgar signals to Nelly that she must fetch servants to assist in expelling Heathcliff. Clearly stirred by the two men fighting for her affection, Catherine locks Edgar and Heathcliff in a room together. Edgar cowers and shows terror, while Heathcliff displays only contempt. Heathcliff escapes and Catherine orders Nelly to tell Edgar that she is ill. Edgar tells Catherine that she must either relinquish Heathcliff or him and demands that she make a choice. Catherine dismisses Edgar from her presence.

Key point

The confrontation between Edgar and Heathcliff (pp.113–116) signals a clash of Catherine's two loves and their different values. Clearly excited and agitated by the conflict, Catherine seems to enjoy watching the two men fight over her (although Edgar's performance is somewhat pathetic). This marks a turning point in Catherine and Edgar's marriage, but also in Catherine's tentative grasp on life – realising that she must choose between Edgar and Heathcliff, she opts out of the decision by making herself ill.

Q Analyse Catherine's response to the confrontation that she brings about by locking Heathcliff and Edgar into a room together (p.114). Referring to the text, consider why she is so excited and agitated by the conflict.

Volume I, Chapter XII (pp.120–133)

Summary: *Catherine makes herself dangerously ill, while Isabella elopes with Heathcliff.*

Catherine shuts herself away and, with the exception of a basin of gruel, she declines to eat – starvation, for Catherine, is a significant nervous reaction. She behaves feverishly and yearns to be on the moors or at Wuthering Heights. Edgar enters the room and is horrified by Catherine's haggard appearance. He blames Nelly for not keeping him informed of his wife's illness. Nelly then finds Isabella's spaniel hanging from a wall and learns from Mr Kenneth that Isabella had pledged to elope with Heathcliff. It is obvious that Heathcliff is responsible for the act and his cruelty towards the dog signals that Isabella is well aware of his brutality. Nelly discovers that Isabella has already gone, but decides not to inform anyone, leaving a young servant to discover her absence. Edgar is warned that Catherine's life is in danger unless she can be kept calm, although the doctor later modifies this warning to suggest that it is Catherine's sanity that is in danger, rather than her life. Edgar announces that he has disowned Isabella.

Q Nelly conceals a great deal of information in this chapter. Why does she do so and what effect do her concealments have on the narrative and her credibility as a storyteller?

Volume I, Chapter XIII (pp.134–144)

Summary: *Isabella writes to Nelly of the warring atmosphere at the Heights.*

After two months, Catherine's health is declared to be out of danger (she has been suffering from 'brain fever') and we learn that she is pregnant. Isabella writes to Nelly, detailing her fear of Heathcliff and the unpleasant reception she received from Hareton, Joseph and Hindley at Wuthering Heights. Hindley warns her that she should lock the door if she sleeps in Heathcliff's room. Isabella is briefly tempted to use Hindley's pistol against her husband. She urges Nelly to visit her as soon as she is able.

Q Why is it that Isabella cannot simply leave Heathcliff?

Volume I, Chapter XIV (pp.145–153)

Summary: *Nelly visits the Heights and is alarmed at the change in Isabella.*

Nelly tells Edgar of the letter and passes on Isabella's desire for forgiveness to Edgar, who responds coldly. Nelly visits the Heights, where she is dismayed to see that Isabella has already begun to neglect her appearance – a reaction to her ill-considered marriage. Nelly informs Heathcliff that Catherine's illness has changed her and warns him not to seek an interview. Heathcliff speaks of Isabella with contempt and indicates that she is his prisoner. In spite of her earlier assertion that Heathcliff should not make the attempt, Nelly agrees to help him see her, believing that he may bring about a 'favourable crisis' (p.153) in Catherine's illness.

Q In this chapter Heathcliff is extremely vocal about his revenge plot, yet his cruelty is at odds with the child who had imagined heaven with his playmate, Catherine (p.44). How plausible do you consider this change in Heathcliff's character to be?

Volume II, Chapter I (pp.157–165)

Summary: *Catherine and Heathcliff are reunited.*

Although she knows that Heathcliff is lurking near the Grange, Nelly delays handing his letter to Catherine, again making a choice that impacts upon the events to follow. Heathcliff and Catherine are reunited in a scene notable for Heathcliff's passionate intensity. Heathcliff expresses his anger towards Catherine for her betrayal of their love and weeps when Catherine speaks of her death. He blames her for choosing Edgar and social and material ambitions over him. Linton returns to find Heathcliff, but is distracted from his rage by the fact that Catherine has fainted. Nelly is characteristically unsympathetic towards Catherine, believing that it is 'so much the better' (p.164) if the incident has killed her. Nelly persuades Heathcliff to wait outside, thus avoiding a confrontation with Edgar, who is torn between concern for Catherine and anger towards his rival.

Key point

Catherine and Heathcliff meet and speak of their great passion (pp.160–163). The scene is laden with pathos because Catherine is so close to death and also because Heathcliff blames her for causing their suffering by betraying their love. Knowing that he will have to live without her, Heathcliff thinks of the difficult future he will face. He also, uncharacteristically, weeps and thus shows the extremes of his violent emotions.

Q Think about Nelly's role in this chapter. Do you warm to her as a flawed narrator or do you experience difficulties with her account? Explain your response with reference to the text.

Volume II, Chapter II (pp.166–170)

Summary: *Cathy Linton is born and Catherine Earnshaw dies.*

Catherine (Cathy) Linton is born at midnight and two hours later her mother dies, without regaining consciousness. The hour of Cathy's birth is in keeping with the novel's Gothic elements, yet it is misleading in that the little girl's character is considerably sunnier than that of her mother.

Nelly expresses what might seem to us a somewhat macabre fascination with watching in 'the chamber of death' (p.167). However, death was much more present in the nineteenth-century consciousness as life expectancy was much shorter and mortality rates were considerably higher. Nelly once again shows her aversion towards Catherine by suggesting that she did not deserve a 'haven of peace at last' (p.167) and shocks Lockwood by asking whether people such as Catherine can be happy in the afterlife.

Nelly eventually gathers the courage to tell Heathcliff that Catherine has died and he responds with terrifying vehemence, dashing his head against a tree and demanding to be haunted. While Edgar keeps a watch over Catherine's open coffin in the days leading up to her burial, Heathcliff keeps a parallel vigil outside the Grange. When an exhausted Edgar finally leaves the room, Nelly interferes once more by leaving a window open to allow Heathcliff to enter the Grange. Nelly returns later to find a curl of Edgar's hair that Heathcliff has discarded from Catherine's locket and replaced with a lock of his own. Nelly twists the locks together, creating an artificial unity. Catherine is buried on the moor and, although Hindley is invited, he does not attend. As a result, Edgar is the only mourner who is not a tenant or servant, pointing to the isolation of Catherine's life. Drawing us back to the present, Nelly also remarks that Edgar now lies next to Catherine in a simple grave, thus reminding us that we are listening to a narrative of past events.

Q Why is Catherine buried on the moor and not with her ancestors or in the Linton family plot?

Volume II, Chapter III (pp.171–188)

Summary: *Catherine is buried on the moors and Isabella escapes from the Heights*

Nelly comments that the Friday of Catherine's burial signalled a shift in the weather – from fine days to a month of rain, sleet and then snow. The bleak weather symbolises the emotions of the characters who are mourning Catherine. Brontë uses this device (known as 'pathetic fallacy') at a number of other key moments in the novel.

While nursing baby Cathy, Nelly is disturbed by Isabella, who has escaped from Wuthering Heights. Isabella agrees to dry herself and change her clothes before she leaves. Having told Nelly of the violence and misery of her life at the Heights, Isabella is driven away in a carriage and never returns. A few months after her escape, Isabella gives birth to her son, Linton Heathcliff, whom she reports to be 'an ailing, peevish creature' (p.183). Thirteen years later Isabella dies, leaving twelve-year-old Linton in Edgar's care.

After Isabella's death, Nelly explains, Hindley dies (outliving his sister by only six months) and Joseph suspects that Heathcliff was involved in his death (p.187). Hareton is left a beggar as his father died while in debt to Heathcliff. Nelly is horrified at the degradation Heathcliff heaps upon the child and asserts that she will take Hareton back to the Grange with her. Heathcliff responds by threatening that if she removes Hareton, then he will assert his legal claim over Linton. Hareton is then reduced to the state of depraved ignorance and dependence in which Lockwood finds him on his first visit to the Heights.

Q Can you identify passages, both in this chapter and in the novel as a whole, where the weather is more than just a backdrop? What are the characteristics of these passages and how does Emily Brontë use the weather to draw attention to her characters' feelings?

Volume II, Chapter IV (pp.189–198)

Summary: *Cathy leaves the grounds of the Grange and Nelly finds her at Wuthering Heights.*

Nelly glosses over the first twelve years of Cathy's childhood, noting that although she is equally intense in her attachments, Cathy's character is gentle and soft, and that she is not at all like her mother. Edgar keeps Cathy in ignorance of Heathcliff and the world of the Heights, and she does not leave the grounds of the Grange until she is thirteen. While Edgar is away, collecting Linton Heathcliff after his mother's death, Cathy becomes restless and rides her pony over the hedge and away from the Grange. When Nelly finds her, she has made her way to Wuthering Heights, where Hareton and the housekeeper persuade her to rest when her pony and dog are bitten by the working dogs of the Heights (here, again, there is a contrast between Cathy's spoiled pet and Hareton's labouring animals).

Cathy is offended by Hareton's familiarity when she learns that he is a dependent and Hareton in turn responds with embarrassment and aggression. The housekeeper shocks Cathy by revealing that Hareton is her cousin and Cathy reveals that Edgar has gone to collect Linton.

Showing her characteristic desire to avoid being reprimanded for her negligence, Nelly persuades Cathy to conceal her visit from her father, explaining that she could lose her position.

Q Have Nelly's character and judgement developed since the beginning of her story?

Volume II, Chapter V (pp.199–203)

Summary: *Edgar brings Linton to the Grange, but Heathcliff claims the boy immediately.*

Linton Heathcliff arrives at the Grange showing a 'sickly peevishness' (p.200) owing to his delicate health. Spoiled and cosseted, Linton is too concerned with taking care of himself to engage in any of the frivolities of childhood. Edgar's fears that Heathcliff will claim his son are substantiated when Joseph arrives to collect the boy. Edgar refuses to hand him over, protesting that he will be his guardian, but Joseph warns that unless Linton is surrendered, Heathcliff himself will come to collect his son.

Q Why do you think Heathcliff wishes to claim Linton?

Volume II, Chapter VI (pp.204–210)

Summary: *Nelly takes Linton to Heathcliff. Linton is shocked to learn that he has a father.*

Fearing that Heathcliff will arrive at the Grange, early the next morning Edgar dispatches Nelly to Wuthering Heights with Linton. When Linton asks about his father, Nelly lies to him, downplaying the conflict between Heathcliff and the Lintons, and telling him that Edgar and Cathy will visit him. Both Joseph and Heathcliff are shocked at Linton's effete appearance, with Heathcliff going so far as to ask, 'Where is *my* share in thee, puling chicken?' (p.207). Heathcliff divulges his plot to use Linton to take possession of Thrushcross Grange, while Nelly believes that she can console Edgar by telling him that Heathcliff understands Linton's delicate health and the need to treat him gently. Linton cries in terror when Nelly attempts to slip away, insisting that he will not stay in the house.

Q Why is Heathcliff so disappointed in Linton?

Volume II, Chapter VII (pp.211–228)

Summary: *On her sixteenth birthday, Cathy goes to Wuthering Heights, where she finds Linton.*

Cathy is distraught when she discovers that her cousin has gone and Edgar attempts to placate her by pledging that Linton will return soon, but adds that he *may not* be able to get him back. Nelly meets the housekeeper from Wuthering Heights, who makes a number of complaints regarding Linton's delicacy.

On her sixteenth birthday, Cathy drags Nelly outside to see moor game and, with Edgar's permission, they leave the confines of the park. Cathy rapidly leaves Nelly behind and is apprehended near the Heights by Heathcliff and Hareton. Heathcliff persuades Cathy to enter his house, tempting her by saying that she knows his son. Nelly attempts to resist and voices her concern that Edgar will blame her for this incident. Heathcliff outlines his plan that the cousins should fall in love and marry. Although he has carefully planned his bid to take over Thrushcross Grange, Heathcliff regrets that Linton is so sickly and voices his admiration of Hareton, believing that he would be a much more worthy son.

Nelly and Cathy return to the Grange, where Cathy immediately tells her father of the visit and reproaches him for concealing Linton's whereabouts. Edgar explains his feelings towards Heathcliff, offering a brief summary of the role he played in her mother's death and emphasising that he does not want her to return to the Heights. Nelly later finds Cathy crying for her cousin and upbraids her for her foolishness. Although Nelly forbids her charge from corresponding with her cousin, she later discovers that Cathy and Linton have secretly exchanged a number of letters, and that Cathy believes herself to be in love with her cousin. Once again concealing matters from Edgar, Nelly agrees to remain silent if Cathy will allow her to burn the letters.

Q Do you think Nelly should have concealed Cathy and Linton's letters from Edgar? Does the fact that she did change your attitude towards her as a character and/or as a narrator?

Volume II, Chapter VIII (pp.229–235)

Summary: *Heathcliff persuades Cathy to visit Linton.*

Edgar falls ill and Cathy voices her fear of being left alone, while Nelly attempts to manipulate her by suggesting that she might kill her father if she continues to pursue a relationship with Linton. Whilst rambling in the park, Cathy loses her hat and climbs over the wall to collect it (as in Jane Austen's writing, the scaling of a wall can symbolise a character's movement to a state of danger). Unable to climb back over, Cathy is apprehended by Heathcliff, who scolds her for failing to write to his son. He then threatens to send Cathy's letters to her father. Heathcliff employs emotional blackmail to persuade Cathy and Nelly to accompany him back to see Linton, claiming that the boy is dying from grief and disappointment.

Q Consider how Heathcliff manipulates Cathy's emotions in this chapter.

Volume II, Chapter IX (pp.236–244)

Summary: *Linton suggests to Cathy that they should be married. Nelly falls ill and is unable to monitor Cathy's whereabouts.*

Upon her arrival at the Heights, Cathy and Nelly find Linton abusing Joseph for neglecting him and it is immediately clear that Linton spends his days complaining. Linton reveals that his father has verbally abused him. He also suggests – at Heathcliff's urging – that Cathy should become his wife. The pair argues over the past and their parents' roles in the drama between Heathcliff, the Earnshaws and the Lintons. Nelly threatens to tell Edgar if Cathy attempts to see her cousin again.

Nelly is then ill for three weeks, during which time Cathy seems to divide her attention between Edgar and Nelly. Nelly notes that at this time she mistakes the colour in Cathy's cheeks as the result of sitting by a warm fire, when in fact they are the result of an evening ride across the moors.

Q Thinking about the symbolism of climbing over walls, consider the significance of Cathy's threat to climb out of the grounds of the Grange if Nelly curtails her excursions to the Heights.

Volume II, Chapter X (pp.245–255)

Summary: *Cathy admits to secret visits to the Heights and Nelly tells Edgar of them.*

When Nelly leaves her sickbed, she is struck by Cathy's restlessness in the evening and realises that she has been to see Linton. Although she initially lies to Nelly, Cathy soon admits that she has visited Linton almost every night for the past three weeks. Cathy describes one of her visits, noting in particular the difficulty of her interactions with Hareton, who retaliates against her teasing by banishing both Linton and Cathy from the fireside to Linton's room. Linton coughs blood and, although he is obviously very ill, continues to use his condition to punish Cathy. The argument escalates and Cathy leaves, cutting Hareton with her whip when he attempts to talk to her reasonably. She then stays away for two nights, before returning to check on Linton's health. Although she does not intend to stay or to repeat her visit, Linton persuades her that it is his poor health that makes him so irritable and the two are reconciled. Cathy explains that she has visited Linton every night since this scene, with Heathcliff keeping his distance, but admits that they have scarcely been happy. Nelly scolds Cathy for her meanness towards her cousin and, while she responds to Cathy's request to conceal the events from Edgar by saying that she will think things over, she betrays Cathy by going directly to her father and telling him the whole story. Edgar forbids any further visits and placates Cathy by saying that he will arrange for Linton to visit the Grange.

Q Compare and contrast Cathy and Linton's different versions of heaven (p.248).

Volume II, Chapter XI (pp.256–259)

Summary: *With Edgar's permission, Cathy and Linton begin to meet on a weekly basis. Nelly misjudges the state of Linton's health, believing him to be better.*

Nelly explains to Lockwood that the events she has narrated took place just over a year ago. She suggests that Lockwood might fall in love with Cathy and he responds in a characteristically panic-stricken manner.

Continuing with her story, Nelly explains that Cathy kept her promise to her father and stayed away from the Heights. Edgar, knowing that his death is looming, expresses concerns about Linton's worthiness as a husband for Cathy. As his health deteriorates, Edgar invites Linton to the Grange and Linton responds (in a letter that shows Heathcliff's input) with the suggestion that they might meet on land near the Heights. Unable to accompany his daughter because of his ailing health, Edgar refuses, but a correspondence begins. Cathy and Linton beg to be allowed to begin weekly rides or walks together under Nelly's supervision. We also learn that Heathcliff has been ill-treating Linton.

Q What effect does Brontë achieve by allowing Lockwood's voice to intervene at this point in the narrative?

Volume II, Chapter XII (pp.260–264)

Summary: *Linton's ill health casts a pall over his meeting with Cathy.*

Linton and Cathy meet. Linton is feeble and unable to travel far, yet he denies that his illness and his temperament have deteriorated still further. It becomes clear that the boy is terrified of Heathcliff. Cathy is bitterly disappointed with her cousin's self-absorbed behaviour. Nelly, who now thinks that Linton's health is worse, advises Cathy not to relate this fact to her father, believing that they will learn more after a repeat visit.

Q How does Linton reveal his fear of his father?

Volume II, Chapter XIII (pp.265–277)

Summary: *Heathcliff imprisons Cathy and Nelly at Wuthering Heights. Cathy learns that she is to be married to Linton.*

Edgar's health is in decline and while Edgar hopes that Cathy will be relieved of her sorrow through her meetings with Linton, the encounters are clearly an ordeal for the petulant, sickly young man. Cathy berates Linton for his lack of engagement in their meetings. Heathcliff appears and makes light of his son's illness, even though he knows that, like Edgar Linton, the boy is dying. Heathcliff asks Cathy to walk Linton home. Nelly and Cathy are imprisoned at Wuthering Heights and Heathcliff responds to Cathy with violence when she attempts to escape. Linton reveals to

Cathy that they must be married. Cathy pleads to be allowed to return to her dying father but is taken away, while Nelly is left locked in Zillah's room at the Heights for five days, with Hareton as her jailer.

Q Look at Cathy's interactions with Heathcliff. To what extent does her behaviour evoke memories of her mother?

Volume II, Chapter XIV (pp.278–285)

Summary: *Edgar Linton dies.*

Zillah returns to the Heights and sets Nelly free. Upon learning that Edgar is still alive, Nelly determines to go to him, but she is unable to persuade Linton to let Cathy – who is now his wife – go to her father. Nelly attempts to appeal to Linton's conscience, but he refuses to co-operate, instead detailing how he plans to make Cathy suffer. Nelly leaves for the Grange alone and finds Edgar still alive. Edgar tries to secure Cathy's inheritance before his death, but we later learn that the lawyer he has engaged, Mr Green, has been bribed by Heathcliff. Cathy escapes and is able to see her father one last time.

Volume II, Chapter XV (pp.286–291)

Summary: *Cathy and Nelly are separated. Heathcliff looks upon Catherine's face again.*

Cathy and Nelly hope to be allowed to stay on at the Grange after Edgar's funeral, but Heathcliff tells them that he plans to let the house to a tenant and wants Cathy to live at Wuthering Heights. Nelly asks to be allowed to change places with Zillah, but Heathcliff declines the request. Heathcliff tells of how he opened up Catherine's coffin and saw her face once more, unaltered by death, and recalls exhuming her the day after her death so that he could hold her once more. This experience marks a turning point for Heathcliff, whose obsession with revenge gradually begins to yield to a desire to return to Catherine.

Q Consider the importance of memory to Heathcliff in this chapter. How do memory and haunting become entwined with each other?

Volume II, Chapter XVI (pp.292–298)

Summary: *Linton Heathcliff dies. Hareton tries to befriend Cathy.*

Nelly comments on Zillah's difficult relationship with Cathy, reporting the results of a long talk with the housekeeper six weeks ago. Linton Heathcliff dies after Heathcliff refuses to call a doctor, while Zillah does nothing to help. Heathcliff inherits all of Linton's property, which includes the lands that should rightfully be Cathy's. Hareton tries to help Cathy and, in a scene reminiscent of Heathcliff's request to Nelly to make him look decent, Zillah helps to make Hareton presentable. Hareton asks Cathy to read to him, but is met only with contempt. Lockwood announces his plan to spend the next six months in London.

Q Compare Cathy's response to her husband's death with Heathcliff's reaction to that of Catherine Earnshaw.

Volume II, Chapter XVII (pp.299–304)

Summary: *Lockwood goes to the Heights to announce his departure.*

Lockwood takes a note from Nelly to Cathy at the Heights. He finds Cathy sullen and miserable. Hareton intercepts the note, but returns it to Cathy, who explains that she has nothing to read and no writing materials because Heathcliff and Hareton have taken them. Cathy ridicules Hareton's efforts at self-improvement and Hareton burns her books. Lockwood informs Heathcliff of his impending departure.

Q Heathcliff has attempted to turn Hareton into the degraded creature that Hindley made him as a child. Examining this chapter, how successful have Heathcliff's efforts been?

Volume II, Chapter XVIII (pp.305–316)

Summary: *Lockwood finds Cathy and Hareton engaged to be married.*

Lockwood finds himself near Gimmerton and decides to spend the night at Thrushcross Grange. He learns that Nelly is now the housekeeper at Wuthering Heights and goes there to visit her. Upon his arrival, he is surprised to see Cathy reading with Hareton – the two are obviously on affectionate terms. Lockwood regrets what he regards as his missed opportunity to woo Cathy. Nelly tells him of Heathcliff's death three months before and explains how Cathy and Hareton have become close, partly because an accident has left Hareton housebound. We learn that the pair will marry soon.

Q How plausible do you find Cathy's relationship with Hareton?

Volume II, Chapter XIX (pp.317–325)

Summary: *Hareton and Cathy become close friends, while Heathcliff loses his extraordinary energy.*

Nelly continues telling Lockwood of what happened prior to Heathcliff's death. Cathy is giddy with happiness at her new friendship with Hareton and Nelly warns her against letting Heathcliff know of this development, but the young woman is unable to conceal her happiness. Cathy taunts Heathcliff, but in spite of the violence he has shown towards her in the past, he is curiously unable to follow through on his rage. Hareton's loyalties are divided by the confrontation and he is upset by Cathy's abuse of Heathcliff. In a particularly disturbing moment, Heathcliff sees Catherine Earnshaw's eyes when Cathy and Hareton look up at him. He tells Nelly that he has lost the urge to live and spurns food and drink. Joseph is furious when Hareton pulls out bushes to make a flower garden for Cathy.

Key point

The vision of Catherine's eyes unsettles Heathcliff and becomes an almost supernatural experience.

Q Why does Heathcliff lose his impulse for revenge just when he seems to have achieved everything he set out to do?

Volume II, Chapter XX (pp.326–337)

Summary: *Heathcliff dies, Cathy and Hareton are to be married, and Lockwood leaves.*

Heathcliff continues to behave strangely, avoiding people and hardly eating. His conduct is out of character and echoes Catherine Earnshaw's self-starvation in the first volume. Nelly is terrified by Heathcliff's appearance and compares him to a goblin (p.329). This chapter is saturated with Gothic imagery, most of which originates with Nelly, who asks whether Heathcliff is a 'ghoul, or a vampire' (p.330) and who becomes so fixated on him that she dreams of him. Realising that Heathcliff is heading towards death, Nelly attempts to make him aware of his sins. He spurns her religious overtures and seems uncannily drawn towards Catherine. The weather changes and brings heavy rain (which often represents death), and Nelly finds Heathcliff's dead body in Catherine's chamber, with the window open. Nelly characteristically conceals Heathcliff's starvation from Mr Kenneth, who is puzzled by his death. Heathcliff is buried next to Catherine on the moors and, though a local child believes he has seen a ghost, Nelly remarks that she thinks the dead are at peace.

Q What effect does Emily Brontë achieve by surrounding Heathcliff with Gothic imagery in the run-up to his death?

CHARACTERS & RELATIONSHIPS

Characters are listed in order of appearance.

Lockwood

Key quotes

'"If the little fiend had got in at the window, she probably would have strangled me!" I returned. ... "I'm not going to endure the persecutions of your hospitable ancestors again ... And that minx, Catherine Linton, or Earnshaw, or however she was called – she must have been a changeling – wicked little soul! She told me she had been walking the earth these twenty years: a just punishment for her mortal transgressions, I've no doubt!"' (p.27)

Lockwood is the narrator who initiates the story of Catherine and Heathcliff. Although most of the tale is recounted by Nelly Dean to regale Lockwood when he is ill, it is his voice that passes the story on to us. The narration is particularly complex in that Lockwood's voice gives way to Nelly's for most of the story, only appearing from time to time to remind us of this complex framing device. While Lockwood represents himself as misanthropic, he finds the solitude of the moors to be oppressive and begins by pressing himself upon Heathcliff's company. Lockwood, who has moved to the north after a failed flirtation, proves himself to be a poor judge of character. At the novel's beginning, he somewhat comically identifies himself with Heathcliff, even though their two characters could hardly be more opposed.

Nelly Dean

Key quotes

> '"Worthy Mrs Dean, I like you, but I don't like your double dealing," he added, aloud.' (p.233)

It is Nelly's voice that we hear for most of the story. The same age as Hindley Earnshaw, Nelly is a girl when the events that she describes begin and a 'stout' woman in her forties when the story ends. Nelly is a fallible narrator and we are invited to question her judgements and decisions, particularly in relation to Catherine Earnshaw, whom she confesses to having disliked. Nelly thinks of herself as a steadfast and loyal servant. However, she frequently withholds information from other characters: she fails to tell Catherine that Heathcliff is listening to her confession that she will put social ambition above love by marrying Edgar Linton (vol. I, chapter IX); and she decides not to inform Edgar Linton of the severity of his wife's illness (vol. I, chapter XII). She also interferes in a number of situations, as is exemplified by her lie when she tells Heathcliff that Edgar is not part of the group of men coming to expel him from Thrushcross Grange (pp.115–116). Although she betrays Cathy Linton's trust when she reveals Cathy's secret visits to Wuthering Heights to Edgar (p.254), Nelly loves Cathy and is delighted by her engagement to Hareton Earnshaw at the end of the novel.

Joseph

Key quotes

> 'Th' divil's harried off his soul ... and he muh hev his carcass intuh t' bargin, for ow't Aw care! Ech! what a wicked un he looks girnning at death!' (p.335)

An elderly retainer who speaks in an almost incomprehensible dialect, Joseph represents an austere brand of Christianity with no scope for forgiveness. He shows hostility to all of the characters, although he possesses a small degree of loyalty to Hareton and the Earnshaw name.

Catherine Earnshaw

Key quotes

> 'Nelly, I *am* Heathcliff – he's always, always in my mind – not as a pleasure, any more than I am always a pleasure to myself – but, as my own being ...' (p.82)

A passionate, headstrong child, Catherine is indulged and unruly before Heathcliff's arrival and becomes even wilder when she forms an allegiance with Heathcliff. As a young woman, Catherine is torn between the luxurious life of leisure she experiences at Thrushcross Grange and the need to be true to her heart. Catherine's determination to marry the mild and malleable Edgar Linton in spite of her deep love for Heathcliff reveals an element of her character that repeatedly leads her to hurt herself. Having learned about social hierarchy at the Grange, Catherine remarks that it would 'degrade' (p.81) her to marry Heathcliff and she yields to her worldly ambitions by choosing to marry the wealthy and handsome Edgar.

Catherine is a willful young woman who responds to crises by becoming ill and who seeks to hurt those around her by harming herself. Her illnesses, the second of which is described as a 'brain fever' (p.134), are both tied to an unwillingness to eat. She repeatedly threatens to take her own life if it will cause Edgar pain (pp.120 and 128). Catherine is unsuited to the genteel life at the Grange and, when she falls into a delirium, she yearns to be out on the moors where she can be free or back at the Heights.

Hindley Earnshaw

Key quotes

But, I thought in my mind, Hindley, with apparently the stronger head, has shown himself sadly the worse and the weaker man. When his ship struck, the captain abandoned his post; and the crew, instead of trying to save her, rushed into riot, and confusion, leaving no hope for their luckless vessel.' (p.185)

'Jealous of Heathcliff from the day of his arrival, Hindley deeply resents his father's preference for the foundling. The story's multilayered narration prevents us from gaining a great deal of insight into Hindley's psychology, but it is clear that he feels displaced by his rival. Like Catherine, Hindley is able to form passionate attachments, as is exemplified by his love for his wife, Frances. He is, however, just as stubborn as his sister, as he demonstrates when he refuses to accept the doctor's verdict on his wife's health (p.65). Following Frances' death, Hindley loses his own will to live. Neglecting his son Hareton, he seeks solace in drinking and gambling, and becomes even more tyrannical in his behaviour.

Heathcliff

Key quotes

'I have no pity! I have no pity! The more worms writhe, the more I yearn to crush out their entrails! It is a moral teething, and I grind with greater energy, in proportion to the increase of pain.' (p.151).

Heathcliff is a mysterious figure whose origins are the subject of speculation and whose motivations are not always obvious. Nelly suggests that Heathcliff may be son of the 'Emperor of China' (p.58), but the fact that Mr Earnshaw finds him at the port of Liverpool points to Irish ancestry (Eagleton 1995, pp.1–26). The mystery surrounding his origins is never resolved and adds to the enigma that is Heathcliff's character.

The younger Heathcliff shows few signs of the vengeful tyrant that he is to become and, although he is hardened and unwilling to show any sign of suffering when Hindley beats him (p.38), he is also mischievous and playful in his exploits with Catherine. As a boy, Heathcliff is prepared to take advantage of Mr Earnshaw's favouritism, threatening and manipulating Hindley into exchanging horses with him when his colt is lamed (p.39). Heathcliff is tenacious and determined, and initially struggles hard to keep up his education, although the demands of the hard physical labour imposed on him by Hindley eventually make this impossible (p.68).

Although she says that she gains plaudits for taking care of Heathcliff when he is dangerously ill with the measles, Nelly admits that she is unable to 'dote' on Heathcliff and is slightly mystified by Mr Earnshaw's affection for him (p.39).

The young Heathcliff is tough and obviously accustomed to abuse, but nothing prepares the reader for the way his character changes during his three-year absence. John Sutherland registers the change when he comments, 'When he returns to Wuthering Heights after his mysterious three-year period of exile Heathcliff has become someone very cruel. He left an uncouth but essentially humane stable-lad. He returns a gentleman psychopath' (Sutherland 1998, p.53). The Heathcliff who leaves is sensitive enough to keep a record of the time Catherine spends with Linton, as compared to the days she spends with him (p.70). Moreover, his departure signals that he is wounded by Catherine's assertion that it would degrade her to marry him. The Heathcliff who returns obviously remains passionately attached to Catherine, but has become devious, brutal and vengeful during his time away. Heathcliff's cruelty extends to violence against women: he is brutal in his treatment of Isabella (pp.182–183) and he strikes Cathy (p.281). His viciousness towards Isabella's spaniel (p.129) demonstrates the force of his anger and his mercilessness towards even the truly defenceless.

In the novel's final pages, Heathcliff's character undergoes another unusual shift when he loses the impetus for revenge and, indeed, for life. Having blazed with energy and fury for so much of the novel, this sudden change in his character is unexpected and, for some readers, a little implausible. His refusal of food and his yearning to be reunited with Catherine through death are, nevertheless, consistent with the force of his character and the extremes of his emotions.

Frances Earnshaw

Key quotes

'She was rather thin, but young, and fresh complexioned, and her eyes sparkled as bright as diamonds. I did remark, to be sure, that mounting the stairs made her breathe very quick, that the least sudden noise set her all in a quiver, and that she coughed troublesomely sometimes …' (p.45).

Married to Hindley, Frances is a slight, delicate character whose fear of death is obvious from the moment of her arrival at the Heights. We learn nothing of her origins, which leads Nelly to surmise that she does not have a fortune or a well-connected family to recommend her (p.45). Nelly describes her girlish delight in the house and suggests that she exhibits hysterical behaviour during the preparations for Mr Earnshaw's funeral (p.45). The source of Frances' anxiety soon becomes apparent when she falls ill and dies, behaving with a 'gay heart' (p.65) to the last.

Edgar Linton

Key quotes

'Whatever our souls are made of, his and mine are the same, and Linton's is as different as a moonbeam from lightning, or frost from fire.' (p.81)

Initially depicted as a spoiled young man, fighting with his sister over a lapdog (p.48), Edgar gradually changes from an infatuated young man to a loving and devoted father. He shows himself to be a kind husband in his willingness to humour Catherine (p.92), yet it is also clear that he is too weak a character to stand up to her headstrong behaviour. Edgar behaves in a cowardly manner when confronted by Heathcliff at Thrushcross Grange (p.115) and although he obviously loves his wife, his affection appears insipid when compared with Heathcliff's great passion. Edgar's character develops, however, and instead of indulging in a protracted period of mourning for Catherine, as Hindley does for his wife, Edgar becomes an affectionate and responsible father. Edgar's reclusiveness after Catherine's death is an extreme response to his grief. The fact that he cuts himself and his daughter off from society causes problems when Cathy eventually encounters Heathcliff and the world of the Heights.

Isabella Linton

Key quotes

> 'Is Mr Heathcliff a man? If so, is he mad? And if not, is he a devil?' (p.136)

Although she is a spoiled and petted child when we are first introduced to her, as an adult, Isabella shows great patience with her tempestuous sister-in-law Catherine, seeking to placate her and giving way to her demands (p.92). Isabella mistakes Heathcliff's brutality for Byronic heroism and, in spite of Catherine's warnings, she demonstrates a romantic naivety in her decision to elope with him.

Once her illusions about her marriage have been shattered, Isabella's conduct and appearance deteriorate so rapidly that Nelly is shocked and Heathcliff describes her as a 'mere slut' (p.149). Although the moral universe of the Heights is blurred, Isabella continues to show scruples in refusing to allow Hindley to kill Heathcliff. She also demonstrates a tenacity that is unexpected, given the comfort of her former life at the Grange, when she escapes from Heathcliff and runs all the way back there, before fleeing to the south of England.

Hareton Earnshaw

Key quotes

> '... he'll never be able to emerge from his bathos of coarseness, and ignorance. I've got him faster than his scoundrel of a father secured me, and lower; for he takes a pride in his brutishness.' (p.219)

Hareton is the son of Hindley and Frances Earnshaw. Frances' death, a short time after his birth, leaves Hareton entirely in Nelly Dean's care. However, this arrangement is short-lived and, when Heathcliff takes up residence at the Heights, he begins to take his revenge on Hindley by degrading the boy in the same way that Heathcliff himself was demeaned. In spite of Heathcliff's efforts, Hareton never gives way to the bitter, vengeful behaviour that characterises his oppressor and Heathcliff acknowledges this when he speaks of his admiration for the boy, compared with the contempt he feels for his own son, Linton (p.219).

While Hareton's coarseness shocks Cathy, Lockwood recognises that he is not what he seems during their first encounter, when he notes the haughtiness of his bearing (p.12). Although he is uninstructed, Hareton possesses an innate intelligence and sensitivity, which lead him to show kindness to Cathy in spite of her rudeness towards him. He is also instinctively generous towards Lockwood and is willing to help him when bad weather leaves him stranded at Wuthering Heights (p.17). Outstandingly loyal, Hareton feels affection for Heathcliff and, despite the latter's crimes against both himself and Cathy, Hareton mourns the older man's death.

Catherine (Cathy) Linton

Key quotes

> 'She was the most winning thing that ever brought sunshine into a desolate house ... Her spirit was high, though not rough, and qualified by a heart, sensitive and lively to excess in its affections.' (p.189)

The daughter of Catherine Earnshaw and Edgar Linton, Cathy displays repellent behaviour when Lockwood meets her in the opening chapters. However, we soon learn that this conduct is a result of Heathcliff's ill-treatment. Cathy is loved deeply by her father Edgar and, although she is accustomed to having her own way in most matters, she does not share her mother's bad temper. Much more a Linton than an Earnshaw, Cathy's love (both for her father and Linton) is strong, but it is not destructive. Although she is imperious at times, particularly when speaking to Hareton, she is a good-natured young woman, as is demonstrated by her eventual willingness to teach the rough young man to read.

Linton Heathcliff

Key quotes

> '... Linton requires his whole stock of care and kindness for himself. Linton can play the little tyrant well. He'll undertake to torture any number of cats if their teeth be drawn, and their claws pared.' (p.274)

Linton is a sickly, ill-tempered young man. It is difficult for the reader and the other characters to determine whether Linton's illness is responsible for his petulance or whether it is the result of his mother spoiling him. He also lacks strength of character. Linton is seldom happy and seems to take most delight in taunting Hareton Earnshaw for his ignorance. His illness is sufficiently serious to kill him, and he is not averse to exploiting it to gain sympathy and to make Cathy do his bidding (pp.252 and 253–254). Terrorised by Heathcliff, Linton is unable to assert himself against his father and, although he eventually aids Cathy in her escape from the Heights to see her dying father, he is, according to Heathcliff, vocal in his desire to punish Cathy (pp.287–288).

THEMES, IDEAS & VALUES

Birth, class, lineage and revenge

In spite of the turbulence of the characters' passions and the extremes of the Yorkshire weather, *Wuthering Heights* is a novel that is deeply concerned with order and its restoration. When Lockwood arrives at the Heights, he remarks on the house's age, noting both the date '1500' and the name 'Hareton Earnshaw' above the front door (p.4). At the time of Lockwood's visit, the house is, of course, in Heathcliff's hands, since he has taken it from Hindley Earnshaw as part of his revenge against him.

The plot of *Wuthering Heights* revolves around the turmoil that ensues following Catherine Earnshaw's decision to place social and material ambitions above passion by marrying Edgar Linton. Her actions are the catalyst for Heathcliff's revenge scheme, which involves denying Hareton Earnshaw his birthright – the ancestral home – and thus disrupting the order of inheritance within the Earnshaw family. In exacting his vengeance on the next generation, Heathcliff continues the chaos that Catherine started and, having begun the novel without any property of his own, he is bent on stripping inherited wealth away from those around him.

William Empson rather flippantly suggested that, '*Wuthering Heights* is a good case of double plot in the novel ... telling the same story twice with the two possible endings' (in O'Gorman, p.222). The pattern of repetition seeks to reverse the damage caused by the first Catherine while moving towards a more conventional, conservative form of closure. The repeated and muddled names within the drama constantly remind us of the original characters, as well as the historical length of the Earnshaw family line. The fact that Hareton cannot read his family name and the date above the front door reveals the extent to which Heathcliff has robbed him not only of his inheritance, but also of his identity as an Earnshaw. Importantly, Heathcliff himself has only one name because his origins are unknown. Therefore, Hareton's learning to read marks an important movement from being like his single-named oppressor to claiming his heritage and the property that rightfully belongs to him.

Cathy Linton begins the story with her mother's married name. She later becomes Catherine Heathcliff – the name that her mother should have had – when she is forced to marry Linton and then finally reverts to her mother's maiden name through her marriage to Hareton. The fact that both of her marriages are to her cousins highlights the claustrophobic world of the novel, but it also suggests an ultimately conservative view about lineage and its disruption. The Earnshaw family was almost ruined as a result of Mr Earnshaw bringing an outsider, the 'cuckoo' Heathcliff, into the household and by Catherine's marriage to Edgar (p.35). In aligning herself with her cousin, Cathy restores her family's unity, brings together the fortunes of the Earnshaws and the Lintons, and rules out the possibility of an alliance with an outsider, such as Lockwood.

Marriage

When it was first published, one of the most scandalous aspects of *Wuthering Heights* was the cavalier attitude of the first generation of characters towards their marriages. At a time when divorce was frowned upon and difficult to get, Isabella's elopement with and subsequent flight from Heathcliff would have cast her in an unfavourable light, in spite of Heathcliff's abhorrent cruelty.

Marriage is problematic in the world of *Wuthering Heights* and, for most of the characters, it comes to represent entrapment. While Catherine naively believes that she can use Edgar's wealth to assist Heathcliff, in reality her marriage sparks a deadly rivalry. Heathcliff's return shows Catherine that she has made the wrong choice and emphasises the extent to which she is constrained by the comfortable yet dull life she leads at Thrushcross Grange. Her only escape from its bonds is through death – a solution that is characteristically drastic and dramatic.

The most horrific of all the marriages is that of Isabella and Heathcliff. Although Isabella behaves with naivety in refusing to see Heathcliff as the villain he truly is, her decision to elope with him is the result of misinterpretation. Like so many nineteenth-century women in fiction and in fact, Isabella is unschooled in the ways of the world and misreads Heathcliff's brooding nature and violent tendencies as a type of dark, Byronic masculinity. The scenes that take place when Isabella returns with Heathcliff to Wuthering Heights are graphic in their physical and psychological violence. When Heathcliff prevents Isabella from leaving, it is only because he wishes to exact his revenge on Edgar by ill-treating his sister (p.151). He admits to the most excessive cruelty when he declares to Nelly:

> ... I've sometimes relented, from pure lack of invention, in my experiments on what she could endure, and still creep shamefully cringing back! ... I have avoided, up to this period, giving her the slightest right to claim a separation; and what's more, she'd thank nobody for dividing us – if she desired to go she might – the nuisance of her presence outweighs the gratification to be derived from tormenting her! (p.150)

Here, Heathcliff confesses not only to using force against his wife to test her endurance, he also admits his complete indifference towards her. He declares that he has made sure that Isabella will not be able to obtain a divorce: nineteenth-century law favoured husbands and Isabella would have to prove both cruelty and desertion in order to be legally separated from him.

Linton Heathcliff is no better a husband than his father. His weakness prevents him from causing any serious harm to Cathy, but he makes it clear to Nelly that he regards his wife as his chattel, laying claim to her possessions and expressing pleasure when Heathcliff strikes her (p.281). While Nelly assures us that Cathy and Hareton will be married (later on), thus offering us the prospect of a happy ending, it is worth noting that in a novel where so many marriages have gone awry, we do not witness the couple's wedding.

An unconventional heroine

Although the story begins in 1801 and flashes back to the previous century, it was written during the 1840s, when gender relations for the middle classes were governed by what was known as the 'separate spheres' ideology. Space was divided into the 'public' and the 'private', with the former representing the outside world of the streets and the workplace and the 'private' constituting the home. While men were able to negotiate the two spheres and move between them, women of the middle and upper classes were largely confined to the domestic 'private' space. Women were expected to resemble the subject of Coventry Patmore's 1854 poem, 'The Angel in the House', ministering to their husbands and creating a home that offered sanctuary.

Catherine Earnshaw, with her wilful personality and explosive temper, certainly never fits this model and this makes her very different from the more acceptable, passive, girlish heroines of novels such as Charles Dickens' *David Copperfield* (1850), for example. The difference between Catherine and the ethereal, charming heroines of contemporaneous works is obvious even in her earliest years. As a child, the first Catherine does not experience any difficulties in expressing her feelings or making others aware of how she feels. However, after her accident and her stay at Thrushcross Grange, self-expression becomes more difficult for her.

As Sandra Gilbert and Susan Gubar point out, after the Lintons take in Catherine, her relationship with authority and patriarchy is redefined (Gilbert and Gubar 1979, p.302). Gilbert and Gubar make much of the fact that Catherine loses blood before she enters the Grange, arguing that symbolically this represents the onset of puberty and forces her to become aware of gender boundaries for the first time. Up until this point, she and Heathcliff 'promised to grow up as rude as savages' (p.46), living in an almost Edenic state on the moors, where hierarchical social and gender codes do not apply.

The Catherine who scampers across the moors is dynamic and active, but during her weeks at the Grange she becomes a much more static figure. Whereas at the Heights she has been able to rule Heathcliff by command, at the Grange she learns that if she is to be accepted into its world of privilege, she must adhere to a far more rigid set of conventions that will not allow her to do as she pleases. Just as Catherine undergoes a change of temperament in response to a world where she may not do as she pleases, she also transforms her appearance to become a 'dignified person' (p.53).

This 'taming' of wild Catherine Earnshaw is, of course, temporary. While Catherine may assume the clothing of a fine lady, she is unable to completely subdue her imperious nature, which resurfaces in the scene where she pinches Nelly, shakes Hareton and then slaps Edgar (p.71). After her marriage, although Catherine believes that she makes concessions for the benefit of Edgar and Isabella, Nelly tells us in no uncertain terms that they yield to her every demand (p.92). During Heathcliff's absence, Catherine's conduct is exemplary, but as Nelly asks, revealing her impatience with the indulged Mrs Linton, 'who *can* be ill-natured, and bad-tempered, when they encounter neither opposition nor indifference?' (p.92).

Heathcliff's arrival creates a crisis for Catherine and, from this point onwards, she is no longer able to submit to the behavioural codes of the Grange. Nelly tells us that 'our fiery Catherine was no better than a wailing child' (p.124) in the wake of Edgar's confrontation with Heathcliff. However, Catherine's tears and illness are a long way from the passion and violence of her temper in the novel's early chapters. This suggests that she is struggling to express her true feelings, torn as she is between the propriety demanded of her as Edgar Linton's wife and the deep feelings she has for Heathcliff. Catherine's strong emotions make her an extremely unconventional Victorian heroine, leaving Emily Brontë little choice other than to let her to die, since she cannot be comfortably contained within a respectable home.

Illness and starvation

When Catherine returns from Thrushcross Grange, Hindley's wife, Frances, becomes a kind of mentor to her, endeavouring to teach her how to behave and dress in a ladylike fashion. The delicate, consumptive Frances is an odd role model for the assertive and robust Catherine, but she is, nevertheless, influential, as it is from her that Catherine seems to learn a new form of self-expression – the art of being ill.

Elaine Showalter has commented on the empowering nature of illness for some women:

> Deprived of significant spheres of action and forced to define themselves only in personal relationships, women have become more and more dependent on their inner lives, more prone to depression and breakdown. Sickness offers a tempting escape from the contingency of the feminine role; it offers a respectable reason to be alone, and real, if perverse, opportunities for self-development (Showalter, p.64).

When Catherine returns from the Grange, her days of running around in as grubby a state as Heathcliff are over. One of her first acts is to contrast her new gentility with his ever-increasing degradation by laughing at how dirty he looks and his sulky demeanour (p.55). Catherine now reacts to Heathcliff's maltreatment not by joining him in overt physical rebellion, but in more circumspect ways. When Heathcliff is banished from the festivities on Christmas Day, she is unable to eat and hides her emotions by diving beneath the table. She is still sufficiently like her old self to climb into Heathcliff's garret (attic) to be with him, but this episode points to a growing conflict between the two worlds that Catherine now inhabits. She has gained an awareness of the limitations imposed by society and knows that she cannot make a display of her emotions in front of the Lintons.

When Heathcliff leaves (an abrupt response to Catherine's assertion that it would degrade her to marry him), Catherine responds with the first of a sequence of self-induced illnesses that mark a new form of (socially acceptable) protest. Beyond a childhood attack of the measles, Catherine has never really been ill, but her experience at the Grange and her daily contact with Frances give her a new experience of sickness. At the Heights, illness is treated as an inconvenience to be shaken off as quickly as possible, as exemplified by Hindley's insistence that his wife will recover, even when she is on her deathbed (pp.65–66). The Grange, however, is a place where invalids are indulged and become the centre of attention.

Catherine returns from her first stay at the Grange physically better, but with a fractured identity and the realisation that illness and injury will gain her both attention and sympathy. Perhaps it is for this reason that when Heathcliff absconds, she makes herself ill by standing out in the rain, 'wandering to and fro ... in a state of agitation' (p.85). By making herself ill, Catherine is punishing herself for her role in Heathcliff's departure, but she is also – through a complex process of displacement – punishing Heathcliff, too. His body is absent, so she takes revenge on the body that is closest to his – her own. Having declared to Nelly that she *is* Heathcliff, Catherine seems to subconsciously register that she can do her hardened friend more damage by harming herself than by attacking him.

Catherine's married life at the Grange is ostensibly an easy one, with the Lintons submitting to her every whim. However, for a character who had previously taken such delight in conflict and self-expression, this period of 'sunshine' (p.93) is likely to have been tedious, which may explain the 'seasons of gloom and silence' that she experiences (p.92). With the Lintons bending to her every whim, Catherine is denied an outlet for her strong emotions, which she then turns on herself. Heathcliff's return acts as a reminder to Catherine of the freedom her previous life offered and that she really does not belong in the prison-like enclosure of a drawing room. Catherine acknowledges as much when she offers to have two tables laid in the parlour (p.95).

Heathcliff's return also reminds Catherine of the agonies she suffered during the early stages of their separation and, following his confrontation with Edgar, she reverts to the state she was in when he left. She feigns illness very vividly by dashing her head against the arm of a sofa and then grinding her teeth. Since she has told Nelly of her intention to manipulate Edgar through shamming, her behaviour is not taken seriously to begin with. However, her conduct soon becomes alarming and raises serious questions about her state of mind:

> ...her hair flying over her shoulders, her eyes flashing, the muscles of her neck and her arms standing out preternaturally. I made up my mind for broken bones, at least; but she only glared about her, for an instant, and then rushed from the room (p.118).

Here, Catherine's illness becomes a type of performance that mutates into a more personal need to unleash emotional tension. It is no longer sufficient for Catherine to merely pretend to be ill; she once again makes herself sick, but this time through deliberate starvation and self-will. Maud Ellmann comments:

In *Wuthering Heights* the themes of hunger and imprisonment are so closely interwoven that they virtually become synonymous with one another. Whenever Heathcliff is incarcerated, Catherine starves; the two motifs converge in Catherine's eerie cry, 'Ellen, shut the window. I'm starving' (Ellmann 1993, p.91).

Catherine's starvation is a response to her separation from Heathcliff and is, as Elaine Showalter suggests in a broader discussion on women who refuse to eat, 'the desperate communication of the powerless' (Showalter, p.5).

Catherine's refusal to eat is partly a response to what she regards as Edgar's negligence and her efforts to starve herself are part of an attempt to punish him. Later, having broken her fast, Catherine immediately regrets her actions, exclaiming:

> Oh I will die ... since no one cares anything about me ... If I were only sure it would kill him ... I'd kill myself directly' (p.120–121).

By the time Edgar is admitted to her presence and the true extent of her illness is revealed, it is too late and Catherine has detached herself from him altogether. In her delirium, Catherine talks about freeing herself from the 'shattered frame' of her body and, with no other viable outlet for her rage, she consumes herself. Catherine's self-starvation begins as a form of empowerment, but it transforms into self-harm and points to the dangers of denying such a feisty, impassioned young woman an outlet for her emotions.

Dogs, class and sublimated violence

The animals in the novel are mostly dogs. How they are treated and their behaviour are often important indicators of people's characters. Lockwood's lack of good sense is apparent when he does not heed Heathcliff's warnings and is attacked by Juno and the sheepdogs (p.7). Brontë uses this scene to show the contrast between Lockwood's life, in which dogs are kept as pets, and the world of the Heights, in which dogs are fierce workers. Unaccustomed to receiving guests, Heathcliff's dogs, like their owner, are unable to behave appropriately when someone from the outside world visits. On Lockwood's second visit, he is detained by the dogs when Joseph thinks he is stealing a lantern, and then when he stays the night he is warned against entering the yard, where the dogs are unfettered.

At Thrushcross Grange, Catherine and Heathcliff witness Edgar and Isabella fighting over a lapdog, which points to the Lintons' moral weakness at this point in the narrative. At the Grange there is a clear distinction between dogs that work and dogs that live indoors, pointing to the much clearer class divisions within the genteel household (here as well, servants do not behave with familiarity or sit around the family hearth). Thus, while Edgar and Isabella's lapdog remains idle and stays within the home (just like the Lintons), Skulker, the working dog, protects the Grange from outsiders. Skulker obviously recognises that Catherine should be kept away from the Grange and bites her ankle. However, in doing so, instead of keeping her out, Skulker offers a reason for her to be brought into the home. Interestingly, when Catherine returns from the Grange her attitude towards dogs has changed and when she is greeted by a dog, she 'hardly dared touch them lest they should fawn upon her splendid garments' (p.53).

Heathcliff is clearly associated with dogs in a range of different ways. When Catherine dies, Nelly tells us that he 'foams like a mad dog (p.162), while Isabella taunts him by suggesting that he should lie across Catherine's grave and 'die like a faithful dog' (p.178). Although associated with dogs, wolves and other wild creatures, Heathcliff is extremely cruel to animals, as shown when he hangs Fanny, Isabella's spaniel, before their elopement (p.129). However, later in the novel, Heathcliff's son Linton reveals that this was not an isolated incident when he remarks to Cathy, 'I wink to see my father strike a dog, or a horse, he does it so hard' (p. 281). Heathcliff's brutality towards helpless creatures would mark him as a particularly malicious villain to the nineteenth-century reader. Furthermore, Victorian literary convention dictated that violence be redirected from people to animals. Dogs, in particular, absorbed blows that would otherwise have been discharged onto people and this would have offended sensitive readers. It is, therefore, likely that the incidents Linton reports reflect a similar violence directed towards him by his father.

In the final chapters of the novel, dogs bring about reconciliation. Hareton, who has previously threatened to set Throttler, a bulldog cross, on Nelly, now offers Cathy a terrier as a gift. Although Cathy rebuffs his advances to begin with, the fact that Hareton is able to see a dog as a pet to be offered in a spirit of reconciliation marks both his difference from Heathcliff and his potential for development. While for much of the narrative animals are aligned with violence and bad temper, as the novel draws to a conclusion dogs, like Hareton himself, are restored to their place within the home.

DIFFERENT INTERPRETATIONS

Different interpretations arise from different responses to a text. Over time, a text will give rise to a wide range of responses from its readers, who may come from various social or cultural groups and live in very different places and historical periods. These responses can be published in newspapers, journals and books by critics and reviewers or they can be expressed in discussions among readers in the media, classrooms, book clubs and so on. While there is no single correct reading or interpretation of a text, it is important to understand that an interpretation is more than a personal opinion – it is the justification of a point of view on the text. To present an interpretation of the text based on your point of view, you must use a logical argument and support it with relevant evidence from the text.

The novel's reception

Although it is considered a classic today, *Wuthering Heights* caused a great deal of controversy when it was first published. Some critics were challenged by the novel's originality and voiced their aversion to the plot's interweaving of the real and the supernatural, not to mention the characters themselves. Charlotte Brontë, in a preface written to defend the novel, pondered 'whether it is right or advisable to create things like Heathcliff', before concluding, 'I scarcely think it is' (p.liii), suggesting that even she had some difficulty accepting and understanding her sister's demonic hero.

A reviewer in *The Examiner* commented in January 1848 that 'this is a strange book' and went on to consider the character of Heathcliff:

> Heathcliff may be considered as the hero of the book, if a hero there be. He is an incarnation of evil qualities; implacable hate, ingratitude, cruelty, falsehood, selfishness, and revenge (in Allott 1974, p.220).

While the reviewer is obviously perplexed by Emily Brontë's creation, he understands literary origins better than some critics, explicitly connecting Heathcliff back to Byron's brooding pirate in *The Corsair* (1814). Another anonymous reviewer in *The Spectator* complained that 'the incidents are too coarse and disagreeable to be attractive' (in Allott 1974, p.217). The review is short and lacking in detail, noting similarities between the works of Acton, Ellis and Currer Bell, but doing so only to dismiss 'the injudicious selection of the theme and matter' (in Allott 1974, p.218).

Not all of the reviews were hostile. An unsigned article, appearing in the periodical *Britannia* on 15 January 1848, celebrated Emily Brontë's remarkable depiction of the natural world, noting the 'scenes of savage wildness in nature', voicing appreciation of the work's originality and wisely recognising the difficulty in judging such an unusual piece of writing. The reviewer concluded by commenting:

> With all its power and originality, it is so rude, so unfinished, and so careless, that we are perplexed to pronounce an opinion on it, or to hazard a conjecture on the future career of the author (in Allott 1974, p.226).

The Brontës read a number of the reviews and Charlotte wrote to her editor, William Smith Williams, about how she had read a short piece by E.P. Whipple from the *North American Review* to cheer up Emily during her final illness. Whipple begins by commenting of the three Brontës:

> the whole firm of Bell & Co. seem to have a sense of the depravity of human nature peculiarly their own. It is the yahoo [a reference to *Gulliver's Travels*], not the demon, that they select for representation; their Pandemonium is of mud rather than fire' (in Allott 1974, p.247).

Like so many of the earliest reviewers, Whipple is outraged and shocked at what he has read, yet he also recognises the 'uncommon talents' of the author and cannot reconcile the power of the writing with his moral positioning. Emily Brontë's genius was evident even to the most hostile reader, yet it was so different from any other writing of the period that critics had trouble understanding and evaluating it.

Interpretation 1: *Wuthering Heights* is a novel that revels in chaos and turbulence

Wuthering Heights is a novel that challenges conventional boundaries and modes of behaviour. The first volume of the novel, in particular, sets itself at odds with the Victorian realist novel, which generally featured respectable characters and often charted their development from childhood to responsible and successful adulthood.

Catherine and Heathcliff are notable for how different they are from the usual Victorian heroes and heroines. While the romance of Heathcliff's origin as a foundling echoes orphan narratives such as Charles Dickens' *Oliver Twist* (1837), as his character develops, it moves away from the dashing gallantry that often typifies the heroes of nineteenth-century novels to a more disturbing, unique type of monstrosity. Heathcliff's expression of emotion is both graphic and violent, so much so that many of the novel's first readers were offended by his free use of profane language and his amoral behaviour.

Catherine, too, is very different from the demure Victorian heroine of novels by the likes of Dickens, Thackeray and George Eliot. She is able to love two men – albeit very differently – and, in a Victorian context, this would lead readers to have doubts about both her sanity and her morality. Furthermore, her violent outbursts, such as when she shakes the infant Hareton and pinches Nelly (p.72), mark her as very different from the types of domestic angels who appear in other novels of the time. Her temper is unpredictable, her behaviour at times violent and erratic, and while a Dickensian heroine would languish on her sickbed, Catherine grinds her teeth, draws her own blood (p.118) and yearns to be out on the moors.

Catherine and Heathcliff's turbulent conduct is perhaps partly explained by the chaotic nature of their home. As children they frequently spurned the constraints of the home for the freedom of the moors. When Hindley takes over as head of the household, their home becomes a place notable for its disorder and anarchy. Hindley's drunkenness and mood swings as he sets about 'degrading himself past redemption' (p.66) make the Heights a place of terror. Edgar Linton avoids him (p.73) and Nelly tells us that so extreme was Hindley's behaviour that 'the curate dropped calling' (p.66). This is a household in which violence is the norm and where a servant, such as Nelly, can be called upon to swallow a knife (p.74). The most extreme example of chaos at the Heights is, however, when Hindley drops the young Hareton from the top of the stairs. Although the incident is an accident, Hindley's intoxication is so extreme that he cannot see that a small child should not be held over a banister.

Catherine's death only adds to the chaos surrounding the characters since it acts as a catalyst for Heathcliff's terrible plot to take revenge on the next generation of Earnshaws and Lintons. While Heathcliff had already begun to degrade Hareton and had married Isabella to spite Edgar Linton, his plan becomes much more ambitious once he loses Catherine. Patient and systematic in the execution of his plan (as seen in the wedding he brings about between Cathy and Linton), Heathcliff's aim is to create as much turmoil as possible for Hindley and Edgar's descendants. He reveals his enjoyment of the tumult he has caused when he remarks of Linton and Cathy, 'Had I been born where laws are less strict, and tastes less dainty, I should treat myself to a slow vivisection of these two, as an evening's entertainment' (p.270). This comment, made when he has imprisoned Cathy at the Heights to force her to marry Linton, reveals Heathcliff's growing sadism and his desire to disrupt the Linton lineage by marrying Cathy to his invalid son.

It is perhaps Heathcliff's death that presents one of the most disturbing and turbulent aspects of *Wuthering Heights*. In an unexpected plot twist, having succeeded in compelling Linton and Cathy to marry, Heathcliff turns listless and displays a lack of interest in revenge. His changed demeanour brings a new type of chaos to the novel. His slow and, arguably, suicidal move towards death unsettles the other characters just as much as his tyrannical behaviour of the past.

By declining food, Heathcliff takes on one of Catherine Earnshaw's defining characteristics and seems to be attempting to become her. He achieves this state, not just through the manner of his death, but also by arranging for his remains to mingle with hers, bribing the sexton to remove one side of her coffin and of his adjoining one when he is buried beside her (p.288). Heathcliff speaks of having been 'disturbed' by Catherine through night and day over eighteen years, a disturbance that becomes more troublesome in the final days of his life. Catherine's haunting presence, whether real or imaginary, threatens to overwhelm Heathcliff and, ultimately, the only way he can end his grief is by joining her and mingling with her remains.

The chaos and turbulence of *Wuthering Heights* are exemplified by the novel's many premature deaths. Nelly and Joseph are the only characters from the first generation who are still alive at the end of the novel. This points to the extraordinary violence and passion driving the self-destructive protagonists of this most extreme of stories.

Interpretation 2: *Wuthering Heights* is a novel that values order and seeks to see it restored

The first half of *Wuthering Heights* is undoubtedly chaotic as Catherine Earnshaw's betrayal of her love for Heathcliff turns their world upside down. However, in spite of the disorder caused by Catherine's disastrous decision to marry the wrong man, the novel moves towards a restoration of tranquillity. This is represented, at the very end of the novel, by Nelly's belief that the spirits of the first generation of protagonists sleep soundly.

The narrative structure of *Wuthering Heights* is designed to lead the reader through the disorder and confusion of events in the first volume. Nelly and Lockwood offer an important contrast to the impassioned protagonists. In relaying the narrative to us, they represent a calmer, more ordered world than that which they describe. As the principal narrator, Nelly is required to order events and present them to us, and although at times judgemental, her voice always remains calm even when she is describing the most catastrophic scenes. In a world where the main characters seem so much larger than life, Nelly's ordinariness makes Catherine and Heathcliff's emotional extremes more believable, while Lockwood's willingness to accept the story's veracity helps us to suspend our disbelief.

The second volume of the novel is much more invested in peace than the first. Through her juxtaposition of the unstable world of Wuthering Heights with the quiet serenity of life at Thrushcross Grange, Brontë sets up a contrast between the raw passion of those who come from the farmhouse and the quiet reserve of characters from the Grange. While the Heights is associated with all that is wild, the Grange represents refinement and sophistication. As a result, Hareton, although born and raised at the Heights, will move to the Grange after his marriage to Cathy. In doing so, he trades the degraded life that Heathcliff forced upon him for a more leisurely and educated existence.

The novel's repetition and mixing of names can be confusing to some readers, but the names are important indicators of the plot's stability.

Catherine Earnshaw changes her name to Catherine Linton when she marries Edgar Linton and, while it is impossible for her to reverse or undo this action, the author seeks to achieve exactly that. Catherine's daughter, Cathy, begins her life as Cathy Linton, but then, like her mother, marries the wrong person and becomes Cathy Heathcliff. At the end of the novel, she finds real love with her cousin Hareton and, in marrying him she will take on her mother's maiden name and become Cathy Earnshaw. The restoration of the Earnshaw name through marriage allows Hareton to finally claim his rightful inheritance, denied for so long by Heathcliff. However, the fact that the pair has chosen to abandon Wuthering Heights suggests a rejection of the turbulent life they both experienced there.

The characters of the second generation are nowhere near as vibrant or memorable as their predecessors. They are much more conventional and seem much better equipped to function in the real world. Cathy, for example, combines the best qualities of her parents and, while Nelly tells us that her 'capacity for intense attachments' evokes memories of her mother, 'she did not resemble her; for she could be soft and mild as a dove' (p.189). Although he is supposed to be as degraded as Heathcliff, Hareton, too, possesses an innate nobility that no amount of manual labour can remove. As Nelly reports, Hareton's 'honest, warm, and intelligent nature shook off rapidly the clouds of ignorance and degradation in which it had been bred' (p.322), implying that, try as he might, Heathcliff was not able to extinguish Hareton's identity as an Earnshaw.

The novel's final pages convey a spirit of hope despite the misery and despair caused by Heathcliff until just before his death. Cathy Linton no longer displays the 'witch'-like (p.15) behaviour apparent on her first meeting with Lockwood, but instead shows a more conventional, nurturing femininity. While her mother may have flouted gender boundaries, for example by bullying Edgar and forcing him to submit to her will (p.92), Cathy's gentle treatment of Hareton shows that she will be a supportive and loving wife. While Nelly looks forward to a happier life with the newlyweds, Joseph, with his extreme religious fervour, will live out his days taking care of the deserted Heights. Thus, the last representative of excessive emotion is placed in exile and the novel ends, as is customary in Victorian fiction, with a marriage and the prospect of a happy future ahead.

QUESTIONS & ANSWERS

This section focuses on your own analytical writing on the text, and gives you strategies for producing high-quality responses in your coursework and exam essays.

Essay writing – an overview

An essay is a formal and serious piece of writing that presents your point of view on the text, usually in response to a given essay topic. Your 'point of view' in an essay is your interpretation of the meaning of the text's language, structure, characters, situations and events, supported by detailed analysis of textual evidence.

Analyse – don't summarise

In your essay it is important to avoid simply summarising what happens in a text:

- A **summary** is a description or paraphrase (retelling in different words) of the characters and events. For example: 'Macbeth has a horrifying vision of a dagger dripping with blood before he goes to murder King Duncan'.
- An **analysis** is an explanation of the real meaning or significance that lies 'beneath' the text's words (and images, for a film). For example: 'Macbeth's vision of a bloody dagger shows how deeply uneasy he is about the violent act he is contemplating – as well as his sense that supernatural forces are impelling him to act'.

A limited amount of summary is sometimes necessary to let your reader know which part of the text you wish to discuss. However, always keep this to a minimum and follow it immediately with your analysis (explanation) of what this part of the text is really telling us.

Plan your essay

Carefully plan your essay so that you have a clear idea of what you are going to say. The plan ensures that your ideas flow logically, that your argument remains consistent and that you stay on the topic. An essay plan should be a list of **brief dot points** – no more than half a page. It includes:

- your central argument or main contention – a concise statement (usually in a single sentence) of your overall response to the topic (see 'Analysing a sample topic' for guidelines on how to formulate a main contention)
- three or four dot points for each paragraph indicating the main idea and evidence/examples from the text – note that in your essay you will need to *expand* on these points and *analyse* the evidence.

Structure your essay

An essay is a complete, self-contained piece of writing. It has a clear beginning (the introduction), middle (several body paragraphs) and end (the last paragraph or conclusion). It must also have a central argument that runs throughout, linking each paragraph to form a coherent whole.

See examples of introductions and conclusions in the 'Analysing a sample topic' and 'Sample answer' sections.

The introduction establishes your overall response to the topic. It includes your main contention and outlines the main evidence you will refer to in the course of the essay. Write your introduction *after* you have done a plan and *before* you write the rest of the essay.

The body paragraphs argue your case – they present evidence from the text and explain how this evidence supports your argument. Each body paragraph needs:

- a strong **topic sentence** (usually the first sentence) that states the main point being made in the paragraph
- **evidence** from the text, including some brief quotations
- **analysis** of the textual evidence, explaining its significance, and an **explanation** of how it supports your argument
- **links back to the topic** in one or more statements, usually towards the end of the paragraph.

Connect the body paragraphs so that your discussion flows smoothly. Use some linking words and phrases, such as 'similarly' and 'on the other hand', though don't start every paragraph like this. Another strategy is to use a significant word from the last sentence of one paragraph in the first sentence of the next.

Use key terms from the topic – or synonyms for them – throughout, so the relevance of your discussion to the topic is always clear.

The conclusion ties everything together and finishes the essay. It includes strong statements that emphasise your central argument and provide a clear response to the topic.

Avoid simply restating the points made earlier in the essay – this will end on a very flat note and imply that you have run out of ideas and vocabulary. The conclusion is meant to be a logical extension of what you have written, not just a repetition or summary of it. Writing an effective conclusion can be a challenge. Try using these tips:

- Start by linking back to the final sentence of the second-last paragraph – this helps your writing to 'flow', rather than just leaping back to your main contention straight away.
- Use synonyms and expressions with equivalent meanings to vary your vocabulary. This allows you to reinforce your line of argument without being repetitive.
- When planning your essay, think of one or two broad statements or observations about the text's wider meaning. These should be related to the topic and your overall argument. Keep them for the conclusion, since they will give you something 'new' to say, but still follow logically from your discussion. The introduction will be focused on the topic, but the conclusion can present a wider view of the text.

Essay topics

1 Consider the ways in which the characters in *Wuthering Heights* engage in self-harm.

2 To what extent do you regard Nelly Dean as a reliable narrator?

3 Discuss Emily Brontë's use of the Gothic in *Wuthering Heights*.

4 Write an essay on entrapment in *Wuthering Heights*.

5 Consider the role of the landscape and/or the weather in *Wuthering Heights*.

6 Discuss the significance of food and eating in *Wuthering Heights*.

7 Isabella Linton asks Nelly, 'Is Mr Heathcliff a man? If so, is he mad? And if not, is he a devil?' (p.136). Consider Heathcliff's character in relation to Isabella's question.

8 How does Emily Brontë represent gender relations in *Wuthering Heights*?

9 Discuss the importance of the context in which *Wuthering Heights* was written to your understanding of the novel.

10 Write about the narrative structure of *Wuthering Heights*, paying particular attention to the different narrators and their voices.

Vocabulary for writing on *Wuthering Heights*

Byronic hero: Modelled on the behaviour of the Romantic poet, Lord Byron, the Byronic hero flouts convention and is renowned for his magnetic sexuality.

Gothic: Following the conventions of Gothic romances of the eighteenth century (e.g. Horace Walpole's *The Castle of Otranto*, 1764 or Matthew Lewis' *The Monk*, 1796), in which characters (usually heroines) were frequently persecuted by supernatural beings and often pursued through claustrophobic, labyrinthine settings.

Pathetic fallacy: A literary device whereby changes in the weather reflect characters' emotions.

Polyphony: A literary device whereby many voices are used in a narrative. In the case of *Wuthering Heights* this term may be used to consider the ways in which characters' voices jostle for our attention.

Romanticism: A literary movement influenced by the Romantic poets, such as Wordsworth, Coleridge, Byron and Shelley. Some of the key features of Romanticism that feature in *Wuthering Heights* include an emphasis on individual emotions, nostalgia for childhood and an interest in the natural world.

Analysing a sample topic

Consider the role of the landscape and/or the weather in *Wuthering Heights*.

Begin by thinking about the significance of the topic. The question is asking you not simply to identify passages featuring landscape and the weather, but to construct an argument about how Brontë uses the novel's setting to shape our responses to her characters. On one level, the landscape is tied to scenery and location, but you might pay attention to which characters fit into that landscape and which ones inhabit it awkwardly. Equally, *Wuthering Heights* is notable for its vivid descriptions of sudden changes in the weather and you should consider how they relate to characters and events. Does the weather change with the moods of key figures? Do weather conditions alter in the wake of important events?

Now that you have identified the significance of the topic, you should begin to focus your argument by thinking about the textual examples that you will analyse to support your ideas.

The outline below is for an essay arguing that changes in both the landscape and the weather reflect shifts in the drama, as well as the emotions of the central protagonists.

Sample introduction

The importance of both the landscape and the weather in the world of *Wuthering Heights* is evident from the novel's opening pages. The house that gives the novel its title is named after what Lockwood describes as 'atmospheric tumult' (p.4) and it is exposed to the brutal north wind. In a novel where the style of narration offers us opinions about characters' states of mind, rather than insights into their psyches, both the Yorkshire moors and the wild weather play an important role in conveying the depth of Catherine and Heathcliff's feelings. I shall, therefore, argue that Emily Brontë brings together the environment and the elements as a way of exploring the emotional state of her central characters.

Body paragraph 1

- Pay attention to those characters who reflect aspects of the moors – for example, Catherine describes Heathcliff as 'an arid wilderness of furze and whinstone' (p.102). Provide a contrast with the more refined characters, such as the Lintons, who avoid the moors and whose home is surrounded by walled, landscaped parkland.
- Consider Catherine and Heathcliff's strong connection to the landscape around them. As children they play together on the moors, which represent freedom from the restraints of Hindley's tyrannical household (see, for example, pp.46–47).

Body paragraph 2

- Explore how the moors also offer liberation from the domestic space, which Catherine, in particular, finds constraining.
- Discuss how the moors become a space where class and hierarchy are irrelevant. Both Catherine and Heathcliff scamper across the moors with bare feet and what we learn of their time there suggests that it is not burdened by conversation.

- Look at the role the moors play when Catherine is an adult and seriously ill. Pay attention to her yearning for open space and the ways in which it represents childhood, her bond with Heathcliff and a time that was free from the complexities of adult relationships. A key quote to analyse here is the passage beginning, 'I wish I were a girl again, half savage and hardy, and free' (pp.125–126).

Body paragraph 3

- Consider the connections between the environment and the weather. The moorland is exposed to the harsh elements, and Catherine and Heathcliff, the characters most strongly associated with the moors, behave towards each other with a raw emotion that mirrors the tempestuous, unpredictable climate.
- Examine the importance of pathetic fallacy in the novel, paying attention to scenes where changes in the weather set the narrative tone and reveal things about the characters' feelings – examples include the storm that follows Heathcliff's departure (p.85) and the icy weather during Catherine's illness (p.126).
- Think about Catherine, Heathcliff and windows. The waif-like Catherine of Lockwood's dream or haunting begs to be let in, but in life Catherine looks out through windows and opens them, partly to let in the cold, fresh air and partly to feel closer to the moorland (p.126). It is pouring with rain on the night that Nelly finds Heathcliff's corpse and the body is wet because Heathcliff opened the window (p.335), presumably to allow Catherine's ghost in before he dies.

Sample conclusion

Catherine and Heathcliff are inextricably connected to the vast wilderness of the Yorkshire moors. Like the landscape, they cannot be tamed or domesticated and, as I have demonstrated in this essay, their love is as dangerous and destructive as the landscape in which it develops. Through a combination of the harsh, changeable weather and the exposed landscape, Emily Brontë creates a setting that reflects and intensifies the reader's understanding of her central characters' powerful emotions. It is, therefore, a fitting end to the novel that Catherine and Heathcliff – along with the more reticent Edgar – should be buried not in the confines of a churchyard, but on the sprawling moorland where their tombstones will be subjected to extremes of climate that match their own deep feelings.

SAMPLE ANSWER

Isabella Linton asks Nelly, 'Is Mr Heathcliff a man? If so, is he mad? And if not, is he a devil?' (p.136). Consider Heathcliff's character in relation to Isabella's question.

Throughout *Wuthering Heights* Heathcliff is described unfavourably by the other characters, including his beloved Catherine Earnshaw. In spite of the suggestion that there is an evil or supernatural element to his behaviour, Heathcliff remains, for many readers, the 'hero' of the novel and one of its more memorable characters. In this essay I shall consider the extent to which Heathcliff may be regarded as a villain, taking into account how he is represented and by whom, in addition to considering the forces that drive him to his desperate revenge.

In assessing the extent of Heathcliff's villainy, it is important to remember that we see him through the eyes of two narrators. Although Lockwood is shocked by Heathcliff's abrupt manner and lack of hospitality, he is sufficiently engaged by him to want to return to the Heights for a second visit. Lockwood's impressions of Heathcliff are distinctly different from those of Nelly Dean, who is responsible for shaping most of our responses. Nelly acknowledges that she shared the Earnshaw children's aversion to Heathcliff and cast him out onto the landing (p.37); she also comments that she 'couldn't dote on Heathcliff' (p.39) even when he was a young child; and that she found it difficult to understand why Mr Earnshaw was so fond of him. Nelly is, as we discover, a highly partial narrator, with strong preferences for some characters, such as Edgar and Cathy, and violent aversions to others, particularly Catherine Earnshaw.

Nelly's dislike of Heathcliff stems from her resentment of the disruption and unhappiness caused by his arrival at Wuthering Heights. The boy is met with hostility and Nelly admits that she and Hindley 'plagued and went on with him shamefully' (p.38). Heathcliff takes ruthless advantage of old Mr Earnshaw's partiality, but is unable to return his love. Nelly frequently describes him as 'hardened' and, although the mystery of Heathcliff's past is never solved, we assume that his toughness is the result of a harsh and difficult early life.

The physical and emotional abuse that Heathcliff experiences when Hindley forces him into a servant's life are important factors in shaping Heathcliff's character. Hindley's actions make it impossible for Heathcliff to marry the socially ambitious Catherine and they also shape other characters' reactions to him. Mrs Linton describes Heathcliff as 'a wicked boy ... and quite unfit for a decent house' (p.50) and later makes it a condition of their visit to Wuthering Heights that Heathcliff is kept from Edgar and Isabella. We see Heathcliff become an outcast in his own home. He is denied an education and reduced to a dependent's status, thus making it unsurprising that his hatred for Hindley grows.

Heathcliff knows from the moment of Catherine's return from the Grange that Edgar Linton has become his rival. At this stage, however, Heathcliff's reaction suggests resignation rather than fury and a desire for vengeance. When speaking of Edgar, he expresses a yearning to be like him and says to Nelly, 'I wish I had light hair and a fair skin, and was dressed, and behaved as well, and had a chance of being as rich as he will be!' (p. 57). This desire to emulate Edgar in no way prepares us for Heathcliff's later actions or the intensity of his emotions.

When Heathcliff disappears it is because he is hurt when he overhears Catherine complain that it would degrade her to be his wife (p.81). The mysterious silence surrounding the three years of his absence prevents us from understanding all of the forces driving his behaviour. When he returns, Heathcliff is a very different character and his awkward self-consciousness and sullen resentment of Edgar and Hindley have given way to something more passionate and deadly. Though he initially intends to see Catherine, settle his score with Hindley and depart forever, this plan gives way to the much more vindictive desire to exact revenge on those connected to his two rivals. This plot signals a change in Heathcliff's character and, although it could be argued that he wishes to avenge Catherine's death, he takes his first step before she dies when he elopes with Isabella.

Heathcliff's wickedness is most evident in his treatment of Isabella and his frail son, Linton. Both he and Catherine warn Isabella that he is far from the right choice of husband, but she is young and romantic, and misunderstands his brutality. He behaves with extreme sadism when he garrottes her spaniel and, after their marriage, it is clear that he has made good on his threat to harm her 'mawkish, waxen face' (p.106). His treatment of Linton is even worse and Heathcliff terrorises his son with threats of violence and fails to provide the care that the invalid boy needs.

Ultimately, the brutality of Heathcliff's revenge suggests that although he may not be a devil, he is certainly capable of terrifyingly obsessive behaviour. The fact that the story is narrated by Nelly makes it impossible for us to understand Heathcliff's psychology. Furthermore, the gaps in his history make it difficult for us to evaluate his motivations and to understand how his past might have shaped his personality. Heathcliff is a passionate but cruel and merciless man, who exhibits violent extremes of both love and hatred, and who is finally consumed and exhausted by his own strength of emotion.

REFERENCES & READING

Text

Brontë, Emily, *Wuthering Heights*, ed. Pauline Nestor, 2003, Penguin, Middlesex.

Further reading

Allott, Miriam, ed.1974,*The Brontës: The Critical Heritage*, Routledge, London & New York.

Barker, Juliet 2010, *The Brontës* (2nd edn.), Abacus, London.

Corbett, Mary Jean 2000, *Allegories of Union in Irish and English Writing, 1790–1870: Politics, History, and the Family from Edgeworth to Arnold*, Cambridge University Press, Cambridge.

Eagleton, Terry 1995, *Heathcliff and the Great Hunger: Studies in Irish Culture*, Verso, London & New York.

Eagleton, Terry 2005a, *Myths of Power: A Marxist Study of the Brontës* (anniversary edn.) Macmillan, Basingstoke.

Eagleton, Terry 2005b, *The English Novel: An Introduction*, Blackwell, Oxford.

Ellmann, Maud 1993, *The Hunger Artists: Starving, Writing and Imprisonment*, Virago, London.

Garrett, Peter 1980, 'The Victorian Multiplot Novel: Studies in Dialogical Form', reprinted in Francis O'Gorman ed., 2002 *The Victorian Novel*, Blackwell, Oxford.

Gaskell, Elizabeth 1997 (first published 1857), *The Life of Charlotte Brontë*, Dent, London.

Gilbert, Sandra M. and Susan Gubar 1979, *The Madwoman in the Attic: The Woman Writer and the Nineteenth-Century Literary Imagination*, Yale University Press, New Haven, CT.

Kettle, Arnold 1974, *Introduction to the English Novel*, Hutchinson, London.

Miller, Lucasta 2001, *The Brontë Myth*, Jonathan Cape, London.

Moretti, Franco 1993, *Signs Taken for Wonders: On the Sociology of Literary Forms*, Verso, London.

Morris, Pam 2003, *Realism*, London, Routledge.

Stoneman, Patsy 1996, *Brontë Transformations: The Cultural Dissemination of Jane Eyre and Wuthering Heights*, Prentice Hall/ Harvester Wheatsheaf, London.

Sutherland, John 1998, *Is Heathcliff a Murderer? Great Puzzles in Nineteenth-Century Fiction*, Oxford University Press, Oxford.

Adaptations

Wuthering Heights has been adapted in many different media and its story remains enormously popular with both readers and viewers. Patsy Stoneman's *Brontë Transformations* (1996) offers an extensive account of the numerous tributes, revisions and derivatives that the novel has inspired, ranging from Kate Bush's haunting song 'Wuthering Heights' (1978) to Sir Cliff Richard's rather dubious casting as Heathcliff in a musical first performed in 1996. The titles below offer a starting point for those interested in adaptations, but the list is by no means exhaustive.

Film

Wuthering Heights 1939, dir. William Wyler, screenplay by Charles MacArthur and Ben Hecht. The Samuel Goldwyn Company. Starring Laurence Olivier and Merle Oberon. Advertised with the caption 'I am torn with DESIRE … tortured by hate!' this adaptation is regarded as a classic and was nominated for eight academy awards.

Wuthering Heights 1970, dir. Robert Fuest, screenplay by Patrick Tilley. American International Pictures. Starring Timothy Dalton and Anna Calder-Marshall. Although not faithful to the original, this adaptation remains popular and received a lot of attention on its release.

Emily Brontë's Wuthering Heights 1992, dir. Peter Kosminsky, screenplay by Anne Devlin. Paramount Pictures. Starring Ralph Fiennes and Juliette Binoche. This adaptation is unusual in that it incorporates the story of the second Catherine, which is usually omitted in films.

Websites

There are many websites devoted to the work of Emily Brontë and her siblings, but you should exercise caution when using them for study purposes. Try to restrict yourself to sites administered by academic organisations, libraries and museums wherever possible.

http://pressandpolicy.bl.uk/Press-Releases/The-Brontës-secret-science-fiction-stories-4e7.aspx

A link to a number of the famous 'Glass Town', 'Gondal' and 'Angria' stories written by the Brontës as children.

http://www.bronte.org.uk

The Brontë Society and parsonage museum's site, which includes pictures of Haworth, a detailed chronology and discussions of the Brontës' writings.

http://www.victorianweb.org/authors/bronte/ebronte/

A helpful scholarly site that includes contextual discussions and identification of the novel's key themes.